Patches and Beyond

Thomas R. Graddy

iUniverse, Inc.
New York   Bloomington

iUniverse books may be ordered through booksellers or by contacting:

iUniverse
1663 Liberty Drive
Bloomington, IN 47403
www.iuniverse.com
1-800-Authors (1-800-288-4677)

Because of the dynamic nature of the Internet, any Web addresses or links contained in this book may have changed since publication and may no longer be valid. The views expressed in this work are solely those of the author and do not necessarily reflect the views of the publisher, and the publisher hereby disclaims any responsibility for them.

ISBN: 978-1-4401-4335-9 (sc)
ISBN: 978-1-4401-4334-2 (ebook)

Printed in the United States of America

iUniverse rev. date: 06/04/2009

About six years ago I was sitting in a doctors office waiting my turn to get my exposed skin examined for any cancer or any other skin disease when Mary Mazander walked in and sat down beside me. Mary had been in a Toastmasters Club with me, but had taken a leave of absence and I hadn`t seen her for a while. We started talking, and the conversation soon turned to things I had seen and places I had been in my life. Mary stopped me in the middle of a sentence, and said, "Ray why don`t you write a Book?" I said, "Mary I don`t know how to write a book." She looked at me, and said, "all you have to do is write down what you have been telling me." At this point I was called in to the doctors office. As time passed there were others who asked me the same question. After four or five others asked me the question, I began to think that maybe I should give it a shot. While I was still thinking on the subject I was taken to the Saline County Hospital. With a multitude of ailments that almost took my life, I was in a coma for four and a half days and spent the remainder of 25 days recuperating. When I was told what happened during the time I was in the Hospital, I was convinced that the Lord had a reason for leaving me here a while longer. It was then that I began writing this book. More of this part of the story will be found in a later Chapter.

Chapter 1

My story may be typical of any family member that grew up at the time I did. You are invited to come along and share what I consider an interesting life. I was born June 12: 1925: to a family who already had three children, and had four more after me, which made a total of eight, four boys & four girls. My Father was eighteen years older than my mother. He was born and raised near Dyersburg, Tennessee. His family migrated to Arkansas by way of Walnut Ridge, and settled in a small town, named Laura town, where he met and married his first wife. In the following years they were blessed with five children. When his first born was approximately fourteen years old he lost five members of his family in a nine month period, due to an epidemic of Typhoid fever.

Soon after the loss of his family members, he moved west with his daughter and son, through Batesville, Arkansas, to Drasco Arkansas, where he hired out his team of mules and himself to operate a mule-drawn road grader for a company that was transforming an old wagon road to a wider gravel road that would accomodate an automobile, which was new on the scene. This road, which is now known as Highway 92, went from Drasco, Higden, Morganton, and Bee Branch, where it crossed highway 65 and continued to the south west. As the road work slowly progressed mile after mile through Higden, and on westward. They came to a Church with a cemmetary out back, and a sign on the belfry that read [Colony Church of Christ.] This church was approximately three miles north east of Morganton. After looking around the Church building and the cemmetary my father decided to stay there untill Sunday, and attend Church services. He had grown up in the Church of Christ, and he liked what he saw. They found a place to camp near a stream, not far from the Church, and set up the covered wagon for the night.

Sunday morning, they were all up early ready to go to church.

When they arived they went inside found an empty pew, and sat down. When the services were over, people gathered around to greet them, asked them who they were, and where they were from. One man said; I`m Clayton Graddy. and I think I am your cousin. Another man said; I`m Herman Graddy, and I think I`m your cousin also. Someone said; are you planning to stay around here? Before anyone could answer, a tall slender young lady with dark hair pushed her way through the crowd I`m Pearl Boone, and I am inviting you and your two children to come home with me and my Papa and Mama, You can camp there as long as you like, and look at the area to see if you might want to settle somewhere around here. That was how our Papa met our Mother. After a three or four week courtship they were Married and moved into a house in the Hill community, near the General Baptist church. Papa and Mama became members of the Colony Church of christ, and attended services regularly.

Chapter 2

In the latter part of the first year of their marriage, our half brother died of what they thought was pneumonia. Papa had another loss to endure, but later in the year things began to look better when they were blessed with a baby boy November 11, 1918 who they named William Ralph Graddy. Papa told me one time while he was visiting with us, that they were reading a book that had a character in it named Ralph, when they were looking for a name for him. This character was a little boy about three years old, that disagreed with everything that was said to him, and did not want to do anything that anybody told him to do. They named their fist born after the boy in the book, and he has always lived up to his name.

On September 26, 1921 they were blessed with a little girl. They named her Lavada Elgivie Graddy. She was full of life, and always making a fuss about things. When she was a little older she didn`t like to be told what to do, and she would talk back to you when you said something to her that she didn`t like, especially Papa. If he told her something that didn`t sound quiet right to her, she would talk back to him, and it would always get her in trouble. He would tell her, don`t sass me. I Have been told that he whipped her pretty hard a couple of times with a large switch. Someone told me that he did the same thing to Ralph. I guess we all have been guilty of whipping our kids a might to hard sometime or another. On January 7, 1923, they were blessed with another girl that they named Ruby Verva Graddy. She had a more calm disposition than the first two children. She didn`t require as much attention as the others did. She didn`t have to be carried around all the time to be passified. I suppose, she thought that Mama and Papa needed a break.

I want go into any details about their next blessing, that happened on June 12, 1925: it was me, Thomas Ray Graddy. I will tell you more about myself later. On December 14: 1928: they were blessed with

3

another boy that they named Wayne Dale Graddy. Dale was another quiet one. Then on September 3, 1931, they were blessed with another girl that they named Hazel Marvell Graddy. Then they were blessed again on March 3: 1934: with another girl that they named Betty Lois Graddy. They were blessed again on Aug 9: 1936 With another boy, that they named James Archie Graddy. James being the last to be born got more attention than all the others. Somebody was always carrying him around. He never had to wait for anything. You would think he would have been spoiled, and he was, how could you think that he would be any other way?

We were now a family of ten, and we all went to Church every Sunday. We celebrated Decoration Day every spring by cleaning the cemetery and putting fresh flowers on the graves. Then on Sunday we would have all day singing, and dinner on the ground. It was at one of these celebrations that I learned how not to get off of a moving automobile. One of my cousin`s husband had a strip down Ford. He came to the Decoration in it, and I rode with him up the hill to get a drink of water. Later in the afternoon he got into the car and said lets go, I thought he was going up the hill to get water again, I got on with the others, and he started up the road the wrong way. I ask him where he was going, and he said I`m going home, without a word I stood up and stepped straight off the car. when my foot hit the ground the forward momentum spun me around and slammed me broadside against the gravel road. I thought I was badly hurt. but after I laid there a few seconds I realized that I was more scared than I was hurt. I Got up ,brushed myself, off, and realized that I only had a few cuts, and bruises. The thing I hated most, was that my new blue shirt got torn when my elbows hit the ground.

Chapter 3

Papa bought a farm with ninety four acres of land that had forty seven acres cleared for farming. The house was built on a leveled out bench that overlooked the road. A wagon road wound around up a hill behind the house to the field. The barn was located to the west of the house. If you veered off to the left of the road you could drive up by a tall cedar tree that stood at the south West corner of the house ,and on to the barn. I was born in that house a few months after Papa and Mama and the older children moved into it. Growing up on a farm is a good life, even if you don't  realize it at the time. My first memory of my life was when I was about two and a half or three years old. I got my feelings hurt over something that someone said to me, and walked to the far end of the porch where it was dark and sat there until Mama came and told me, come on it's time to go to bed. She picked me up and carried me into the house and laid me on the bed, covered me up and said good night. Life on the farm wasn't easy, you worked from sunup to sundown, and when you got to the barn you had to feed the animals, milk the cows, and do all of the chores you had to do before you could go into the house, wash up and eat supper. That is what they called the evening meal. Of course I didn't have to worry about that until I was bigger. But you didn't have to be very old to chop cotton. I was about seven years old when I started chopping cotton with my two older sisters. I gave my sister Lavada, a hard time. She and my sister Ruby talked to each other while they worked. They could chop faster than I could.

 When they got far enough ahead of me that I couldn't hear them talk, I would stop working and lean on my hoe handle and listen to them talk. Lavada would say; Ray, you better get to work or I'll come back there and give you a whipping, I would just laugh at her, and she would get louder. I knew she wasn't going to whip me, she liked me to much to do that. They would come back and help me catch up. Then the same thing would happen all over again. We look back on it now and laugh about it. Another thing that would get on her nerves was me, standing looking at the sky. Picture a seven year old boy wearing patched overalls, and a straw hat, standing [gazing at the sky.] That was me. I would stand ever so long looking at the sky, especially if there was an airplane flying over. I would watch it from the time I first saw it until it went out of sight. I was fascinated with what I could see, and wondered what was beyond.

Chas, Dale, and, I always found something to do when we didn't have chores to do. There was a rail fence separating Mr. Hagan's pasture from a grove of pine trees. We enjoyed walking the top rail of the fence to see who could walk the longest without falling off. We had a lot of fun doing that until Papa & Mama found out what we were doing. and put a stop to it. They said, don't you know that is dangerous, you could break a leg, back, or neck if you fell of off. We didn't know it was dangerous we replied. It is dangerous, they said, and we're telling you to stay off of it. We did what we was told to do , and stayed off of the fence. When they were out of sight we went into the pine grove and started climbing the trees. When we got up toward the top of the tree it began to sway back and forth. It scared us at first, but we soon realized if we used our body weight we could swing over to the nearby tree. We played for a while ,swinging from one to another. Then we decided to see which one of us could travel the longest distance without touching the ground. Each of us found what we though was the best tree to start with. With the word go; we all started climbing, and climbing, and swinging over to another tree until we must have traveled a quarter of a mile, swinging and swaying, and reaching for the next tree. By this time we were all worn out. We decided it was time to go home. We agreed not to tell anybody what we had been doing.

Chapter 4

We did have time for play. We played marbles, Hop Scotch, jump the rope, hide and seek. We played ball with a home made ball and bat, but that wasn`t very sucessfull, because the ball wouldn`t go very far. But we enjoyed playing it anyway. The thing I enjoyed most was hunting birds with a Bean flip. A Bean flip is a weapon made from a fork of a bush, cut to form a handle to hold in your hand , and the forks extends above your hands. A strip of rubber 12 inches long is attached to the top of each fork. The other end is attached to a length of leather to form a pouch. To fire this weapon, you place a small stone in the pouch and the fork in your right or left hand, and pull the pouch back, to build tension, aim it at the target and release the pouch. The tension fires the stone at the target. It can be deadly up to seventy five yards. You might think we should be ashamed to kill those pretty little birds, but they had the advantage," they could fly, and we couldn`t. Chas Baker who was the same age as me, lived across the pasture from us with his Grandfather and Grandmother, Mr. & Mrs. Hagan. He and I roamed the woods with my younger Brother Dale looking for birds to shoot. We never left home without our Bean Flips. We would have felt like a hunter without his Rifle, without them. Chas couldn`t talk plain. He talked with his mouth open, and it was almost impossible to understand him. Dale and I took it upon our selves to teach him to talk better, and we had him talking a lot better in a few days. We simply told him to close his mouth between words.

When I was six I started to school at the Victory School House, which was located about two miles from our house. In order to get there from our house, we had to climb the hill behind our house, walk across the field, and follow a path down the side of a mountain, across Frank Lewallen`s pasture to a large creek, walk a foot log across the creek, across the road, and on up to the School House. In the winter time, ice would freeze on the grass on either side of the path, making it almost unbearable to travel across the field. We would almost be frozen when we got to School, but there was a pot bellied stove in the center of the room that we could gather around and get warm. There was only one classroom, and one Teacher Miss Nova Hice. Miss Nova taught all eight grades. She was about 5' 4" tall and weighed about 120 lbs, and she could cope with any situation that came up. Those big boys that stood at least a foot above her head didn`t bother her a bit. Miss Nova was my first Teacher and also my favorite Teacher. I finished the third grade there at Victory School.

That was the last year that we went to School there. The school District Consolidated, and I started in the fourth grade at Morganton. I remember my fourth grade Teacher very well. His name was Cowen Boyd. He was a short chubby sort of man with a easy going manner, and easy to like. He taught us to say the Alphabet backwards, and I can still say them backwards almost as easy as I can say them forward. Mr. Boyd was also my Teacher in the fifth grade. It was easy to learn from him. He had a way of explaining things, that made it easy to understand. I enjoyed being in his room, but everything nice has to come to an end. I was passed on to the sixth grade for the next year. In farm country the school term was only seven months long. The fall term started October 1 and ended at the end of April. In most cases, in the fall ,we didn`t get to start to school until the fifteenth of October, and in the spring we would leave school in mid April. If you do the math on this, that makes six months spent in School each year. We made up for one month in Summer School. As we grew older we began to start later in the fall, and quit earlier in the spring. Making a total of five months spent in school. It is very difficult to pass your grades with only five months in school each year. Papa seemed to think it was alright to keep us out of school later in the fall, and take us out earlier in the spring. I had the feeling that he didn`t care weather we went to school or not. There was a girl in my six grade class that noticed that I was having a problem catching up. She asked me if I needed some help, and I said; I sure do. Her name was Winnie Belle Johnson. She asked the Teacher if she could move over, and sit with me so she could help me, and he said; you may. I don`t know what I would have done without her help. Winnie; if you should ever, read this, please know, that I will always be indebted to the girl that took the time to help a classmate. I have told people all through the years about the girl that helped me through grade school.

When I started the seventh grade I found it so much harder to catch up , and keep up, ev en with Winnie`s help I couldn`t do the work that was required of me. I struggled along for a while, and my teacher, Mr. Linn told me that I needed to go back to the sixth grade. I thought about it for a while, and decided to stay out of School for the remainder of the year.   When I started to School the next fall I signed up for the eighth grade, even though, I had missed most of the previous year. I`m sure Mr. Linn noticed what I was doing, but he didn`t say anything. With Winnie`s help I was able to finishing the eighth grade, and was awarded the eighth grade certificate of completion. I considered going to high School, that fall, but my older Sister told me she had tried to go to high School. But she found that she could not catch up after starting so much later than the others.

My older brother Ralph was my hero. He was seven years older than me, and I thought he could do anything. He built a fiddle, using broken pieces of glass, a few old chisels, a hammer, a handsaw, and glue. When he finished the[fiddle,] it looked like a fiddle, it sounded like a fiddle, and it was a fiddle. He used the pieces of broken glass as scrappers to shape the front and back of the fiddle He made a template to shape the edge pieces, and used glue to hold it together. It looked as good as one you would buy in a Music Store. He started working in the woods for Uncle Ant Boone, when he was sixteen years old, cutting bolts that was used to make staves that was used to manufacture barrels. He continued to work for Uncle Ant, any time he wasn`t working on the farm. Ralph got married when he was nineteen years old.

The following spring I was thirteen, and Dale was eleven. I moved up to the two mule#13 Oliver turning plow that Ralph had been using, and Dale took the one mule # 7 turning plow that I had been using. Papa had bought old Sam, the black mule from Jim Pennington some time ago to pull the one mule plow. He was a very good looking mule, big enough to do the job, but he was slow. Papa always wanted us to use both plows on the same land [he called it]. I didn`t understand why he wanted it that way, but he was the boss. When you looked back on what we had done you would see a ridge and a low place, a ridge and a low place. When you have two plows turning the soil on the same land you have a problem. If one   is lower than the other, it inevitable that the faster one will catch up with the slower one, therefore causing a slowdown of the overall project. Dale knew that Papa would not allow that to happen, and used every method he could think of to get old-Sam to move faster. He yelled at him, threatened him, and begged him to no avail. When he got close to the edge of the field, he said whoa Sam.

He walked over in the edge the woods, took out his pocket knife, cut a switch about ten feet long, walked back to the plow, put the lines over his shoulders, and said, get up Sam. Old Sam started walking along at his usual pace. Dale got a grip on his switch, and brought it around with all the force that an eleven year could muster, and placed it on old Sam's side. He flinched a little, and began to move a little faster, Every time old Sam slowed down he heard the swishing sound of the switch, and he would pick up the pace. When he reached the proper pace. Dale fastened the switch to the plow handle, and let it trail behind him. Every time old Sam slowed down, the switch was used again, Dale had a runny nose that day, and had to sniff now and then to keep from dripping. He noticed that when he sniffed old Sam would start moving faster. From then on when old Sam slowed down, he would sniff his nose, and old Sam would pick up the pace. I call that ingenuity.

At the north end of our Farm, the terrain dropped drastically down to a creek that ran along the base of the mountain. Beyond the creek is a ribbon of land that borders the hill beyond, that belonged to Mr. Pea Britton, and his wife Mrs. Britton. Their children had all married, and had families of their own. There were just the two of them left to work the farm. They raised only the crops that would feed themselves,. Mr. Britton took care of the crops in the field, and fed the cows, mules, hogs, and Mrs. Britton took care of the garden, the chickens and household chores. They had a dinner Bell on a post in the back yard, but they never used it, instead she would walk out on the back porch at 12: O clock and call "OOoo Pea OOoo Pea" and he would unhitch his mules, and go the house for dinner.

One day we were chopping cotton at the north end of the field about 11 o clock. We could see Mr. Britton plowing down in his field. Lavada Cupped her hands around her mouth and yelled at the top of her voice, "OOoo Pea OOoo pea", and he immediately unhitched his team and went to the house for dinner. Mr. Britton was well known as the tall tale champion of the county. He bragged about having the fastest buggy horse in whole country. He told the story about him and Mrs. Britton riding along one day and the front wheel came off of the axle, that horse was moving so fast that he reached out and guided the wheel back on the axle with his hand, stopped the horse, went back and got the nut, put it back on the axle, and continued their ride. He could tell those tall tales, one after the other, and she would confirm every one of them, by saying, that`s right because I was right there.

Chapter 5

When I was about seven years old I had a[flock of geese[that roosted in the orchard on top of the hill behind the house. They would fly from the orchard over the house down to the creek that ran through Mr. Hagan's` pasture, get a drink, splash around in the water for a while, and fly back up to the orchard to feed on whatever they could find in the grass that grew among the trees. They would do that several times each day. I enjoyed watching them fly back and forth from the orchard to the creek. They looked so pretty as they flapped their wings, and squawked as if they were talking to each other. I tried many times to show them to my brothers and sisters, but they just couldn`t see them. I guess I had better eye sight than they did.

My favorite thing to do on a rainy day was to day dream. My favorite place to dream was up a stairway off of the back porch that lead to a portico, and on into the attic. I would climb up the stairway and sit on the portico landing and day dream about all the places I would go, and things that I would do some day. I knew there had to be something out beyond the limits of our present day transportation, that I would visit someday, and see all the things and places that I could only day dream about now, I could see myself traveling to other states, and other Countries that I had only read about in books. And some of these things did come true, later in my life.

Chas and I cut wood, hauled it to Morganton, and sold it to a General store owner for a while, but that didn`t prove to be very profitable. We tried working in the hay in the summer but that only lasted about 4 weeks I got a job cutting and pealing high line poles for Harry Chambers. He had bought Mr. Britton's Farm and was harvesting the timber. I teamed up with a guy that was already working for him, and we cut pine trees, cut off the limbs, pealed the bark off with a straightened out hoe for a Dollar a day They were used for high line poles after they were treated with creosote. I used my hard earned money to buy a three year old mare form Harry. I gave him thirty dollars for her. I needed something better to ride than a mule. She proved to be a very good buy. When I put my foot in the stirrup and started to swing my weight up into the saddle, she would take a little turn to the left, and when she felt my weight in the saddle, she would start like rabbit, run like a deer and stop on a dime. She was a pleasure to ride. but when you got on her, you better be ready to ride, I began to ride her to Morganton on Saturday afternoon to get up with my friends, and decide where we would go that night. Sometimes one of the boys could get his fathers truck, and we would all pile in and go to Bee Branch or Clinton to see a movie.

There was a church at Pine Mountain that was about four miles from Morganton that had some good looking girls, sometimes we would ride our horses over there on Sunday afternoon, attend church services, and walk one of the girls home. I walked one girl home that seemed to like me .and I liked her. I asked her if I could come back and walk her home again. She told me I could, I started walking her home regularly. She had a little brother that would take my [mare, ride her home,] tie her to a fence post, and she would be there when got there. That worked out very good. I didn`t have to bother with my mare until we got to her house. One Saturday night Chas and I went to Pine Mountain with a guy in his car. He dropped us off at the Church, went to pick up his girl friend, and brought her to church. When the services were over he took her home and drove back by the Church, and forgot to wait on us, and we had to walk home the long way around because we was not familiar with the short cut. We walked thirteen miles home. On the way we got hungry, barrowed a watermelon from man`s patch walked by his house, sat down, ate the melon and got home at 4:30 in the morning.

Chapter 6

Our only money crop was cotton, and we depended on that crop for money to get us through the winter. We had a good crop of cotton growing, and on August 9.1936. A hot wind began to blow and continued to blow for three days and three nights. When it stopped, the cotton was burned to a crisp. Our money crop was reduced to a field of scraggly looking stalks that would not produce half a bale of cotton. We had to do something to secure money to take us through the winter. Papa hired a man with a truck to move us to Senath Mo, where we could pick cotton. We found a farmer who needed a family to pick for him only. That suited us fine. We picked his whole crop, and made enough money to easily take us through the winter, and had enough left to buy seed and fertilizer for next years crop.

The next year crops were better, but we still went to Missouri to pick cotton again that fall. We made a good amount of money again that fall also. We kept going back each fall, until 1939, our work was cut short by our Mama having an attack of appendicitis, and Papa hired a man to take her to Dr. Rogers in Searcy Dr. Rogers admitted her to the Hospital there. After examining her he told us that her appendix had ruptured, and the poison had spread all over her body. He said he would have to give her medication to kill the poison before he could do surgery. Papa asked how long that would take? Dr. Rogers. Said; it could take as long as three Months. Papa was very quiet for what seemed like an eternity. Then he said; Doctor. I don`t have the money, to pay for her to stay that long in the Hospital. The Doctor. Said; I am building an addition on the Hospital, and you can work for me on the project. I will allow you the going price for your labor, We will arrange for you to eat in the Café, and we will put a bed in your wife`s room for you to sleep on. When this is over, we will see who owes who.

Papa instructed the driver of the truck to take our furniture, and the children home. My older sister, and I faced the biggest challenge of our young lives. At the ages of 14 and 16, we were expected to take on the responsibility of running a farm which entailed, feeding the livestock, milking the cows, cutting wood for the fireplace and cook stove, and hauling it to the house with the wagon & team, carrying wood into the house for the night, and next morning. for the fireplace and cook stove. We agreed, that with Dales help, I could take care of the outside chores, And she and the girls could take care of the inside chores, and all of us would do the washing together. We did the washing, down by the creek in Mr. Hagan's` pasture ,where there was plenty water. We made a game out of it, some of us did one thing, some did another, and we all took the clothes up to the house to hang them out to dry. Not to mention taking the responsibility for the safety, and well being of four siblings. The youngest being only three years old. Ruby and I shared the responsibility the best we could. She being the oldest had the last say.

Mama stayed almost two Months in the Hospital before she was able to have surgery. And it was another Month before she was able to come home. She came home with a tube in her side so the incision could drain. The bandage had to be changed each day. Her recovery was very slow. We were so glad to have her home that we took care of her like a baby. She got better every day, and it wasn`t long until she was doing everything like she always did, full speed ahead.

Chapter 7

In June of 1942 I turned 17 years old, and when crops were laid by that Summer, I left the farm, and went to Little Rock to hunt a job. My sister Ruby had already gotten a job in one of the Defense Plants near Little Rock, and was living in an old Hotel at 9th & main that had been turned into a room and boarding house. She reserved a room for me in the same building, and had it ready when I got there. I came into Little Rock on a Greyhound Bus, and had to walk the 9 blocks to the Hotel. The next morning I was up early, had Breakfast, and started looking for a job. Some one that Ruby knew told me to try the Safeway Warehouse first, and told me how to get there. By the time I got there I had decided that they wouldn`t hire me, and I was a little hesitant to ask, but I walked on in anyway and told them I was looking for a job. They asked me a few questions and told me to come back the next morning at 7:30. The next morning the boss put me with another guy , unloading a box car. We would stack the boxes on a four wheel dolly, seven feet high, push it into the warehouse and stack them even higher than that. We did that all day every day with a short break in the morning and afternoon. I thought farm work was hard, but this was harder. I worked there about two months and quit.

I tried working in the P. X in Camp Robinson for a little while, but didn`t work out for me either. My brother Ralph ask me to come to Bryant and stay with him and his Wife, and get a gob there. I worked in the open pit mines, and drove a dump truck until I went into Service. There was talk about war with Germany as early as 1937, but it was basically speculation. The old folks talked about wars and rumors of wars, and commented on when they thought it would start. When Germany invaded Poland on September1,st that gave them even more to talk about. Then on September 3, 1939, France and Britain declared war on Germany, which made it almost a certainty that the

United States of America would be expected to join in and support France and Britain.

America immediately adopted a voluntary policy to entice young men to enlist for a two year period, with the understanding that they would be discharged at the end of their enlistment period. A lot of young men volunteered for the Armed Services with the thought of serving their two years time, and get out of service, but that was not to be. Only a few of the first volunteers were able to be discharged. On December 7th 1941: Japan attacked America without any declaration of war. Which meant that all of the Soldiers who had volunteered would remain in service for the duration plus six Months. I was only fourteen years old when France and Britain declared War on Germany. I felt sure the War would be over before I would be old enough to be drafted, but I was wrong. Three Months before I was eighteen I received a letter informing me that I should come to the draft Board, and sign up to be drafted into the Armed services. On or before my Birthday, June 12: 1943. In early august I received my notice to report to Camp Robinson on September third to be inducted into the Armed Services of the United States of America. In he meantime I helped my family move from the Farm to Bryant Arkansas. Papa and Mama got work there, and lived there for several years.

Chapter 8

I arived at Camp Robinson late in the afternoon September third, checked in, and was taken, along with other recruits to our quarters by a big burly Sergeant. He gave each of us a number, and said, this is your bed number. Find the bed with your number on it, put your bags on it and, lets go get some chow. When we entered the mess hall we saw a sign that read take all you want, but you must eat all you take. We took our trays off the stack, and slid them along the ledge, each time we came to a server he would dump food on your tray with a ladle. When I saw some food that I didn't recognize, I tried to move the tray so fast he wouldn't be able to dump any on my tray, but he dumped it on the tray anyway. The food in question was cauliflower cooked in a heavy white gravy, and it didn't taste any better than it looked. I ate all around it, and finally had to eat it by itself. I thought I would never get all of it swallowed. We went to our barrack, talked a while and went to bed. At 4:30 the next morning the Sergeant came stomping through the Barracks yelling, rise and shine, grab your blanket in one hand and your privates in the other, run outside and start shaking.

When you get the dust shook off of everything, make up your bed with the top blanket tight enough to bounce a half dollar high enough to turn it over, and report to the mess hall by 5:00 O clock. That was the start of my first day in Uncle Sam's Army. They ran us through all the things that a recruit has to go through the first day in service. In the afternoon they marched us into an area that had bleachers around the perimeter, with a grand stand in the center. An Officer climbed the stairway to the top of the grand stand and began to tell us about the wonderful things that would happen to us in the army. Toward the end of his speech he told us that some of us would have to pull guard duty that night. Then he gave us all the rules of guard duty. The officer of the day was in charge of safety of the camp. The Sergeant of the guard was responsible for taking each guard to his post, and giving him instructions on what to do in certain situations. For instance If some one approaches your post, you are to yell " halt "who goes there, if the person is friendly, ask them to advance and be recognized. The person should state their business. Then you can dismiss them.

He told a story about a guard that was pulling duty on a remote post, when he heard a jeep advancing on his post. He was a little scared, being out there alone. He did what he was supposed to do. He yelled "halt" who goes there, the jeep stopped, a voice answered Officer of the day wife, and bull dog. The guard stayed his ground, and said, Officer of the day advance and be recognized, wife stand fast, bulldog about face and haul _ _ _. I was among those that had guard duty that night. The Sergeant posted me outside of a building that housed German prisoners of war, and gave me an eighteen inch[Billy club to stop any prisoner]who might try to escape. I thought that was the craziest thing I ever heard. What did he think I could do with a billie club that would stop a German Prisoner from escaping.

The second day we were assembled in a building where we would start taking a test on various subjects to find out how smart we were, or maybe how dumb we were. That went on for several days. Then one afternoon the soldier that was giving the test, told us that was the end of the tests., and he was going to start calling names, and when our name was called we could be excused. He began calling names, and one by one they left the room. After about thirty minutes he stopped calling names. I thought, well I guess this is the dummy bunch, but that was wrong. He told us that we had made good enough grades on all the test that we were eligible to take the Army Air Force Cadet Training examination. You could have knocked me over with a feather. I couldn`t believe it. I only had an eighth grade education, and I was going to be allowed to take the Army Air Force Cadet examination?

I didn`t sleep well that night. I was excited about getting to take the test, and fearful that I might fail the test, and I surely didn`t want that to happen. I had always wanted to get in the Air Force, and I hoped that I had the knowledge to answer the questions correctly. I arived at the test room on time, and took a seat close to the test master so I could hear him easily, and waited for the test to start. He appeared from behind a curtain, and asked us to stand, and said; Starting from the front row right you will come by my desk and pick up a copy of the test and go back to your desk and be seated. When every one was seated, he said; You have two hours to complete the test. Most of the questions are multiple - choice questions, and some are yes & no questions, they should be easy. I would suggest that you go through the test and answer those that you know first. Then go back to the beginning and answer each one as you go.

When you finish you may bring your completed test and lay it on the table and you are dismissed for the remainder of the day. You can come by this building and get your test results after 8: 00 A. M. tomorrow. After an hour and a half some of the contestants began to complete the test and leave the building . then one after another they left the building until there were only me and two others, with only minutes left. Then there was only me, with less than five minutes to go. I worked as fast as I could and finished with less than a minute to go. I walked up to the desk and handed my test to the test master, and started to leave the room when he said: wait a minute. You have a few minutes left, and I am, going to check your score before you leave. He laid the test paper over a sheet of paper, and looked at it a minute and said congratulations, [you passed the test by the skin of your teeth.]

I left the building walking on air. I wanted to shout it to the world that I had passed the test that changed me from a soldier in the Army to an Army Air Force Cadet. I couldn`t wait to get back to my barracks where I could write a letter to my folks telling them the good news. We were told that we would be sent to Sheppard field Air Force Base near Wichita Falls Texas to go through 13 weeks of basic training. We arived at Sheppard Field Air Force Base on Friday afternoon, and was assigned to our barracks. We had the whole week end to do as we pleased. Saturday morning we all went to the mess hall and had breakfast. After breakfast we all went out on the exercise field and looked around at all the different things there we were to exercise on. There was a tower with a ladder to climb up, and a rope with knots tied in it to climb hand over hand, and many others I want mention. We all tried out most of them, to see how strong we were only to find how weak we were. We spent the remainder of the week end waking around looking at everything that we were allowed to see, including the airplanes, and wondering which one we would be flying later in our training.

Come Monday morning, everything changed, the fun was over,

the squad Sergeant came into the barracks yelling, hit the deck, you have thirty minutes to get dressed, make up your bed, and be ready to go to the mess hall. From there on we[marched everywhere we went.] When we finished eating we were marched out onto the practice field, and introduced to several different exercises that we would become very familiar with in the following weeks. We practiced every exercise day after day untill we could do them automatically. Then the platoon Sergeant would teach us more things to do, like marching, We started marching on the practice field, then we went on short marches that gradually increased to longer marches untill one day the Sergeant said: Tomorrow is the big day, you guys get plenty of rest tonight, because you will need it. we will be going on a twenty three mile march. I will give you more detailed information in the morning. You are dismissed. The platoon Sergeant marched us out on the field the next morning and halted us at the starting line, and gave us the following instructions. You men have completed several marches of four, eight, and twelve miles. Today, we will march twenty three miles. We will take a ten minute break each hour. During the breaks ,get some rest. It will be up to each of you whether you make the full distance or not. If you make up your mind to go the distance, you probably will, if you have doubts about it, you probably want. Those of you who can`t keep up the pace, get out of the way of the others who can, and wait for the meat wagon to pick you up.

I personally had no desire to ride in the meat wagon, and expressed my opinion of any one who did. Others expressed the same opinion. Then there were others who didn`t care one way or the other. As the hours slowly crept by we began looking forward to the to next break, where we could rest another ten short minutes. We finally reached the half way mark where the Sergeant gave us an extra ten minutes to eat our lunch. When we started back toward camp there was less talk from everyone about going the distance. As the hours went slowly by, I think we all were to the point that we wanted to set down and rest, but we knew that was out of the question. After eight long hours we finely arived at the finish line. We were all very tired, but proud.

Chapter 9

In the meantime we were taking all kinds of Air Force Cadet tests to determine if we were qualified to remain in the Cadet Pilot program. Some of the people that interviewed us must have been psychologists. They would ask you questions that would insinuate that you might have had some kind of weird relationship with your Mother or your Sister. I think it was intended to test your ability to handle insulting remarks without loosing your temper. I don't think I passed the test. We had several other situations that we were subjected to, that was intended to bring out our true character, and build their confidence in our ability to become airplane Pilots. It was at that point in time that I was notified that I had washed out of the Cadet Pilot program. I was not surprised, because I knew in the beginning that I probably didn't have enough education. But I was not badly disappointed. I was still in the Army Air Force, and that is what I wanted in the first place.

When we finished the thirteen weeks of basic training, we were not the same young boys as we were when we arrived at Sheppard field Air Force Base. We were much more than boys who had come from small farms, and towns in Arkansas, and other surrounding States, we were Soldiers. Those of us who had washed out of the Cadet program, became a group that would stay together for many months. It seemed that they didn't know what to do with us. Then one day the word came down to us that we were all going to attend the Airplane and Engine Technical School at Lincoln Nebraska. We were excited about going to technical School, because we could learn a trade, and get a rating for it. But that was not in the cards. The day we arived at Lincoln Nebraska we received word that all technical schools had been closed, because all the allotted ratings had been given out, there-fore there would be no more ratings available untill further notice. That hit us like a ton of bricks. We all had high hopes, only to have them crushed.

We stayed at Lincoln about a month, doing various jobs around the base, doing[K.P duty] and cleaning snow off of the porches and steps of the barracks. The Army volunteered a group of us to clean the snow off the railroad tracks in Lincoln. The snow was more than two feet deep, and I had never seen snow that deep before. It took a lot of work to shovel the snow into trucks that hauled it to the dump. My buddy and I decided to go to Lincoln on Friday night to see what was going on there. We had been wearing boots all weak, and when we walked outside in our low-cut dress shoes to the bus stop to wait on the bus, our ankles froze to the point that we had a problem walking, when the bus stopped to pick us up. Needless to say, we did not stay in town very long. After a few weeks in that climate we eventually grew more accustomed to the colder weather.

We went from there to an air base somewhere in New Mexico, where we entered a weapons school. Our weapons instructor was a colonel, who had won all kinds of shooting matches and had a jacket that was covered with patches he had won all over the world. He taught us how windage and gravity could be factored in to insure more accuracy. He demonstrated this, by pointing out a dark spot on the side of the mountain. He said; that dark spot is a cave. He estimated the distance to be one mile. Using a high powered Army rifle, he set the wind age by estimating the speed of the wind, then he estimated the pull of gravity to set the distance. Then he put a tracer bullet into the rifle, took aim , and pulled the trigger. We could see the curvature of the bullet into the wind, and the arc of the bullet above the line to the target, and saw it enter the dark spot where the Colonel said it would. We were all amazed at what we had seen, and certainly impressed with his knowledge of weapons.

For the next two weeks he taught us about all the parts of a rifle, how to take one apart and put it back together. Then he showed us the proper method to carry the rifle, and the various ways to fire the rifle. Then he had us dry firing the 22 caliber rifle for almost a week before he would allow us to shoot live ammunition. [Dry firing ?] Squeezing the trigger without a live charge in the chamber. The day finally came for us to start firing the 22 caliber for the record. This was a lot more fun. We had a certain number of rounds to fire at 20 yards, and then the target was moved further and further away untill we were firing at long range. At the end of the day I had earned the Marksman Badge. I was enjoying the weapons course very much. But before they dismissed us, they told us we were scheduled to go overseas. They informed us that we would be given a ten day delay in route furlough to Camp Anza California, near Riverside California.

I had been in the Army approximately eight months when I went home on furlough, and I had accomplished very little, but who cares when you are young? When I got home I was informed that my mare had broken out of the pasture and had been picked up by the livestock officials of Alexander, and they were holding her in their livestock pond, with a $30:00 redemption fee. I had to spend part of my precious furlough time to take care of the problem. I spent most of the remaining time with my family, and girl friend Winnie Watts who I dated a few times before I went into the Army. I enjoyed those ten days more than I could say, but as they say, time flies when you`re having fun. I reluctantly said good bye to my family, which was very difficult, because I didn`t know where I was going or how long I would be gone. My brother Dale drove me to the Railroad Station in Little Rock where I boarded the train for Camp Anza California.

The trip to California took three days. About half of that time was spent in the railroad yards, waiting to get out on the main line. When the train got out on the main line it seemed to ramble along with reckless abandon. I enjoyed looking out of the window at the landscape as we moved from one state to another. The scenery seemed to gradually change as we moved through each state, and when we reached the rocky mountains we saw a drastic change in the landscape. The train moved [through deep gorges]where the mountains on each side seemed to reach the ski, with narrow streams running along beside the railroad, which seemed to wind it`s way through the valley like a giant black snake.

After hours of slowly climbing up one long grade, and down the other side, rocking and weaving around tight turns, the train moved down the mountain slopes into the plains of Southern California, where we began to see fruit orchids, as we moved through the country side. I had never been to California before. It was a beautiful scene. We arrived at Camp Anza in mid-afternoon, and was greeted by many of the guys we had been with for several months. We all had stories to tell each other about what we did while we were home, and how nice it was to be with our family again. While we were there my buddy and I went to a gala affair sponsored by the Spanish People in Riverside. All the men and women wore the most beautiful costumes, and the horses wore bridles and saddles such as I have never seen before. The Rumor mill was busy. Every body thought they had the right answer to where we were going, and some of them did have the right answer, but we didn`t know which one untill they told us. As I remember, we stayed there something like three weeks, and the word came down that we would be shipping out in the very near future, but they still didn`t tell us where we were going.

Chapter 10

On June 1 19:44 we were taken by bus to San Diego where we boarded the USS Fredrick Jackson Turner, [A Merchant Marine ship] that was used to ship equipment and supplies to various overseas bases. This particular ship had huge cargo boxes anchored down that covered most of the deck. There was a hold in the middle of the ship that housed 200 Army Air Force soldiers. We cooked, ate, slept and lived in that hold for 63 days. There was space at mid deck where we could move around and get a little exercise. When we had been at sea about an hour the Major in charge, called us together and told us we were headed for China by way of Australia, Colombo Ceylon, and Calcutta India. Most of you have heard of the slow boat to China—Well we were on that boat. Our top speed was 12 knots per hour. There wasn`t much to do except eat, sleep, play cards, and exercise, which we did daily, as a group. Our only bathroom was a rectangular room that was located on one side of the ship with a trough running down each side with slats fastened across it for us to sit on with water being pumped down the troughs that empted out into the ocean. The shower was an enclosure with salt water shower heads, and salt water soap to wash the dirt off with. The soap made a gummy mess out of the dirt. Every week we were allowed to take a bath in the soft water bathrooms the ships crew used.

After a while we got accustomed to our surroundings and began to make jokes about our situation. After all we didn`t have much choice. We couldn`t go anywhere. so we decided to make the best of it. The hold that we ate and slept in had bunks that were twenty four inches wide, and was stacked four high. You barely had enough knee room between you and the man above you. That took a little time to get used to sleeping in such tight quarters. But after a while you could take it in stride and laugh about it. We pulled K.P. [Kitchen Duty] and of course there was always guard duty that had to be done. There were several other holds that were being used to ship supplies to the troops overseas. We soon found out where the refreshments were stored, and we would stand guard while some of us would went down and brought it up on deck .We would hide it and have a party late at night in our hold. The Major would call all of us together and tell us he knew we were stealing things out of the hold, and he would find out who it was, and Court Marshal them, and give them a dishonorable discharge. The Major never did find out how we got the items out of the hold, nor did he ever Court Marshal anybody.

Most of us had never been out on the ocean before, and it was a new experience for us. Every direction you looked there was water as far as you could see. The ship seemed to be sitting in a hole, and when you looked out at a distance it felt as though you were looking up. When we would see another ship in the distance it seemed to be above us, but we soon got accustomed to that. The further we got out to sea the fewer ships we would see. Then there would be days and weeks go by without seeing another ship. We had been out to sea almost a month when one of the ships Officers had an attack of appendicitis, and we had to make a detour to Boro Boro Island where there was a Navy Hospital, and left him there for surgery. When the Captain maneuvered the ship into the bay, we were surrounded with the most beautiful sight I have ever seen. The trees and shrubbery were deep green, the color of the flowers were unbelievable, and the water was a beautiful shade of blue. It seemed that we were caught up in a fairyland of beauty. We dropped anchor and stayed over night there. We were allowed to swim in that blue water as long as we liked.

The next morning the anchor was hoisted and the Captain maneuvered the ship out of the bay into the ocean. We were one small ship in a big ocean again, without an escort. Everybody talked about how beautiful the Island was for several days, and most of us wrote to our folks at home about it as soon as we got to a place where we could mail a letter. The time passed very slowly, but we found things to do, to occupy our minds and body. We had an exercise session daily, and played Pinochle or some other card game. We also had a masseur in our ranks. Everybody was a little reluctant to let him work on them at first, but someone said; You can work on me; When he was finished with him, the guy told us how good it made him feel, then we all wanted to try it. We took turns, and when it came my turn I couldn`t believe how good it felt when he started working on my muscles at the base of my neck, then my shoulders, and down my back. When he finished and I got up off the table I felt that I was twenty pounds lighter on my feet. I could hardly believe that something like that could make a person feel so much better.

Later in our journey we were advised that we were approaching enemy waters, where we were in danger of being torpedoed by enemy submarines. Suddenly we were doing safety drills on how to vacate the hold, and maybe abandon ship. We also were moving into rough waters with waves getting higher and higher, which caused the ship to roll from side to side, [called listing].In the middle of the night it was listing so far that it dumped all the stainless steel trays out on the floor of the galley, which woke us up from a pleasant sleep to a state of fear. We vacated the hold in half the time it took during the drills. When we found out what actually happened we went back down into the hold and cleaned up the mess.

Then one day, word came down that we would be crossing the Equator the next day, and we all would be required to be initiated into the order of Davy Jones who presides over the evil spirits of the deep according to the mythology of sailors. This initiation requires that you run through a paddle line, in the nude, stopping at stations where they do things to intimidate you, for instance, using clippers to cut alphabetic letters across your head that takes months to grow back, and having you to bend over at the last station where they swab you with tar in places that I want mention here. It took weeks to wash that tar off with salt water, We were issued a certificate showing that we had been initiated into The Order of Davy Jones Locker.

A few days after we crossed the Equator we entered the Bass Strait between Australia and Tasmania, where we encountered the roughest waves of all. For eight days the ship [rocked, rolled, and quivered as it plowed into those mountainous waves spraying water from the bow to the stern. We got word from the bridge that the ship was listing up to thirty nine degrees, only two degrees below what it was designed to safely do without capsizing. I pulled guard duty during this time, and from my station by the rail, I could see water within a foot of the top of the rail, and the next moment it would be thirty feet down. I had to move away from the rail because I was beginning to get sick watching

29

the water moving up and down. That was the closest I came to getting see sick during the voyage. When we got through the strait the waves subsided and we began to enjoy the trip again.

Soon after we got through the strait we were told that the ship would dock at Fremantle, and we would be given an over night pass to go ashore and see the sights there. Everybody began to count their money. Some of us already had money enough to go, others began to sell anything they had, to get enough money to get off the ship for just a few hours. We all had high hopes of going into town and meeting some Australian beauty, and spending a few hours with her. But that didn`t happen. The day we arived at Fremantle we were told that the night before we got there, a bunch of British Soldiers and a bunch of New Zealand Soldiers got into a big fight in downtown Fremantle, and the town had been declared off limits to American Soldiers until further notice. I will not try to describe the grammar that was used to voice our disgust. We were very disappointed to say the least. I did get off the ship and set my feet on Australian soil by volunteering to help unload a truck of supplies,[and bring them aboard ship.]

Chapter 11

The Captain maneuvered the ship out of the harbor and headed toward Colombo Ceylon where we joined a convoy headed for Calcutta India. When we reached the point where the Gange River empties into the Indian ocean, we dropped anchor, and waited there for a whole day for the Harbor Pilot to come out and maneuver the ship up the river to Calcutta. The Pilot demonstrated his knowledge of the river channel, by speeding up the river at 15 knots per hour, which was 4 knots faster than it did while crossing the Pacific Ocean. He passed every ship on the river. We walked down the gang plank 63 days after we left San Diego California. It felt good to get our feet back on the ground, even if it was foreign soil. We were loaded into open trucks and hauled to the nearest camp, which was 40 miles north of Calcutta. It rained on us on the way out there. We were all wet from head to toe when we unloaded our duffle bag and carried it into the tent. My buddy Charles Pate and I got our blankets out of our duffle bag and spread them over our cots, realizing that there was no mosquito net around it. We tried to sleep under our blanket and it was too hot. We turned it back, and the mosquitoes started eating on us. I think it would be appropriate to say. We did not get a good nights sleep.

The next day we got our clothes dried, and received mosquito netting to hang over and around our cots. After we got checked in we were able to look around camp. We slept much better the next night. The following night I drew guard duty. The sergeant of the guard took me out into the boondocks to my post, and told me, I will be back in four hours with your relief, and drove off into the darkness. I could hear animals sounds coming from a fenced in area nearby. I could see low buildings in the distance, with dim lights shining through the small windows. As I walked back and forth a feeling came over me that I had never experienced before. I was alone in a foreign country, away from anyone I knew, and for the time, I was home sick.

That was the longest four hours I have ever known. The sergeant of the guard finally came back with my relief, and took me back to my tent, where I could get some sleep. My cot was a wooden frame with a sea grass rope net for the bottom, and a thin pad for a mattress. I got in my cot and fell asleep quickly. Sometime during the night I had something to happen to me that scared the wits out of me. While I was sleeping I laid my left arm out across the wooden rail, and my arm went to sleep. I turned over to the left and my right hand took hold of my left wrist and gripped it. In my half awake state I thought it was somebody else's arm. I jumped out of bed, and landed on the floor , ready to fight anything that was there. Then I woke up. Everybody kidded me about that for weeks. The first week end we were there Charles and I boarded a train to Calcutta. When we got off the train we were surrounded by young Indian kids begging for money, saying boxes saab, boxes saab. We ha been told about the customs of the Indian People, and how we should conduct ourselves. We had also been told that the cow was sacred to the Indians, and if we should see one on the sidewalk we should walk around her.

When noon came we had our first seven course meal at Furpos The most poplar restaurant in Calcutta. After lunch we went to the Jane Temple. We had to pull off our shoes before we went inside. The first thing we saw was the most beautiful chandelier I have ever seen. It must have been ten feet in diameter. Then there were more of the same all through the building. After that we went to the market area. The merchants would meet you at the door and try to sell you something. We were told later that a merchant felt that he had failed as a salesman if he didn't sell you anything. We stayed in town late, and missed our train back to the camp. After a while we met some other guys. One of them was driving a weapons carrier, and asked us to ride back to camp with him. On the way to camp we hit another weapons carrier that flipped us over, spilling us all out on the ground and landed on it's wheels. Outside of some bruises, none of us was hurt. We loaded back into the carrier and went on to Camp.

We learned one thing about the weather there. In addition to it being very hot there, it rained every day. If you went to town, you better take a raincoat with you, because it will rain sometime during the day. It seemed strange to go to the railroad station with a raincoat over your arm with the sun shinning. But, when it started raining you looked right with a raincoat on. We were there about two weeks, and then we boarded a narrow gage train that took us to an Army Base in the northern part of India, where we were scheduled to make preparations to fly over the hump into China. The hump is also known as the Himalayan mountains. This mountain range is the highest peaks in the world which includes Mount Everest that is 29,035 feet tall. There are only a few mountain passes through the range to China.

Chapter 12

On the day we were scheduled to fly the hump [Himalayan Mountains] we were taken to the Army Air Base where we would board a C 46 transport plane that would take us from India to China. The seating consisted of benches on either side, with a parachute for each person to sit on. Above each seat was an oxygen mask. The army slogan is, hurry up and wait, and that is what we did. We waited over an hour before the Pilot and Copilot boarded the plane and started their preflight procedure. Once that was done they taxied out to the runway, and took off. The plane rumbled down the runway forever it seemed, and finally took off into the wild blue wonder, as they say. I might add at this point, that was my first airplane ride. The plane began gaining altitude, and in a few minutes we had gone from boiling hot to freezing. At twelve thousand feet the Copilot came back and told us to put on our oxygen masks. At eighteen thousand feet the plane leveled off for the flight across the mountains. As I looked out the window I could see higher peaks all around me, and I wondered, is this the beyond that I thought about as a boy? When we reached our destination the plane lost altitude too fast , and by the time we landed my ears were killing me. Someone explained to me that chewing gum or working your jaws up and down would dispel the pressure buildup in your ears. I wish they had told me that before. I was on the ground at least two hours before my ears quit hurting.

We were taken up on the hill above the air strip to our quarters We were assigned a bed in a room for four people, me, my buddy and two other guys we had met on the ship. The next morning we were taken down to he airstrip and shown around the Base. There was an Engineering, building, a Quartermaster building, a Maintenance building, and a Motor Pool lined up along the west side of the airstrip. There was a network of streets leading back to six revetments where airplanes could be parked while repairs were being done on them. And further up in the hills there were foxholes already dug to accommodate every person on the Base. They were there in case of an air raid. I don`t want to forget the most important structure of all. The C-46 fuselage nearby that had been turned into snack shop, and it was operated by the Air Transport Command Soldiers, with the help of a young Chinese boy that had been adopted by the Command as their mascot.

After that we were assigned to the maintenance department, who was responsible for refueling all planes that landed on our airfield. Our transportation was a tanker truck and a tug that pulled a six hundred gallon tank. We used these tanks to refuel the planes. When the tanks were empty we refilled them from fifty five gallon drums that was stored in a revetment. It may sound strange but almost half of the gasoline that the planes hauled over the hump was put back into the plane to get it back to India. You might ask, why didn`t they haul it over by truck? The answer to that question was, The Japanese Army closed the Burma Road from India to China early in the War. Almost every plane that landed on our strip was hauling gasoline. After a few days we had learned how to find everything we needed, especially the mess hall and a restaurant behind the Engineering building. The weather was great. At night the temperature would get down to forty degrees. You would need a medium weight jacket if you worked on the midnight shift. In the daytime you could wear nothing more than a shirt.

Soon after we arrived. Charles and I went to a village nearby named U- nan-ye to look around. As we approached the village we were challenged by a guard who stopped us with what sounded like a[grunt] we answered with what we had been told to say. Meg -wy -bing. He waved us by, and we went on into the village. As we walked along the dirt streets we could see eyes peering at us through the dark windows. We walked on as if we didn`t see those eyes looking at us. Soon we came to the market area where every kind of vegetable, and meat was displayed along the curb. I looked at Charles and he looked back at me, with that look that meant, that don`t look good to me either. The Chinese people were smaller than we were and from the way they looked us, they didn`t trust us. We didn`t let that stop us. we went on looking around smiling at them, and before long they were smiling back at us. One man about forty years old spoke to us and told us his name Which I don`t remember, And told us about his wife and four children. He gave us his hone address and asked us to come by and visit him sometime.

The next time we were in the village we went to the address he had given us, knocked on the door, he came to the door and invited us in, and introduced us to his wife and two boys and two girls. His wife was very gracious and offered us something that looked like pastry which we ate, and thanked her for being so nice to us. A few months later we both received a letter from him inviting us to his wedding. After reading my letter I found Charles and ask him what he thought about the invitation, he said; I don`t know what to think, he was married the last time we saw him. We talked it over, and decided to go. On the date of the invitation we dressed in our class A uniform and walked over to the address on the invitation, knocked on the door and waited. The door opened and there he stood, dressed in a suit and tie with a smile on his face. He asked us in and showed us to a big table in the center of the room that was covered with all kinds of food. He asked us to be seated, and motioned for others to be seated around the table. He and a pretty young girl stood at the end of the table, he introduced the girl as his new bride to be. Then they sat down at the end of the table.

The food was passed around the table for anyone to take whatever they wanted . When the chicken platter came around to me, I did a double take. The feet, with the claws still attached was facing me. The head, with the eyes still in the sockets, seemed to be staring at me. My first thought was, they don` t waste a thing, do they? We spent the better part of an hour eating, and sipping rice wine. After eating, I felt like a smoke. I opened a pack of cigarettes, took one for myself and passed them around the table. When they got back to me the package was empty. I`m glad I took one for myself before I passed them around. I don`t think I actually knew when the couple got married. Suddenly everyone was milling around, congratulating the bride and groom. As we were leaving the groom thanked us for coming. We asked him how he could take a wife when he already had one? He said; in china a man can devoice a woman if he wants to do so by saying I divorce you. She has no say in the matter.

We heard there was a flying tigers airstrip about two miles away. Charles and I walked over there one day to see what was still there. There wasn`t much to look at. The buildings were in the last stages of deterioration. We walked down the airstrip over half way and back talking about some of the movies we had seen. If we stopped and listened we could almost hear the roar of a P 40 racing down the strip on take off on a mission to find the Japanese and shoot them down. In my minds eye I could see [William Bendix in the pilots seat]with a big grin on his face. If you listened long enough you could hear them coming back circling the strip and landing one after the other and taxiing up to the strip to the parking area. We walked slowly back toward our own airstrip talking about all the things we had seen and heard about the flying tigers. We agreed that this trip was absolutely necessary.

Chapter 13

As I stated previously. Circumstances beyond my control forced me to leave school after finishing the eight grade. I enrolled in an English correspondence course to further my education, in my free time. After finishing that, I enrolled in another course called the internal combustion engine. I felt that it would give me the knowledge to be an automobile mechanic. I finished it in about three months. Then the Army Air Force offered us an on the gob training program that would allow us to earn a Certificate of Airplane & Engine Mechanic. I enrolled in this course under the instructing of a sergeant, who knew all about airplanes and engines. I worked under him for a few months and became his assistant. As his assistant I was moved up to the rank of Private first class in charge of the engine change crew when he couldn`t be there. I continued in that capacity while I finished the course, and was awarded the Certificate of Airplane & engine mechanic.

Our engineering officer would come around once in a while and to see how we were doing. One time when he came back to see us he said; Graddy, I am trying to get you the rating that you deserve for the work you are doing, the ratings are still frozen, but I think you should have at least a staff sergeants rank for the job you are doing, and I will keep trying. In the meantime you are doing a good job. Every few days he would come back to the revetment where we were working and say; Graddy, 1`m still trying to get you that rating. I would say thank you Captain Fisher. When the war ended in Europe may 8 1945 and the armed services began to send the long timers back to the states to be discharged. Most of the soldiers that went home from our base had a staff sergeants rating or more. Naturally we thought we would get some of their ratings. You can imagine our disappointment when the plane with their replacements landed, taxied up to the operations building, and started getting off the plane. They looked like a herd of zebras walking down the steps. We had a problem being civil to them.

The rank didn`t matter that much. to us, it was the money that went with the rank that we wanted.

It fell my lot to teach a tech sergeant how to do the job that a private first had been doing. It took them longer to learn than it did us .I suppose they wasn`t as eager to learn as we were. But they did eventually finish the course and was awarded the Certificate of Airplane & engine Mechanic. As soon as we finished teaching that herd of zebras, we were told that we were going to Kunming China, which was 137 miles up the Burma road, Also called the Ledo road. The next morning twenty of us loaded our duffel bags on a weapons carrier, and got on a troop carrier and headed east on the Lido road We all had been on a crooked road before, but nothing like this. This road was a gravel road and the roughest I have ever ridden over. We sat on slatted benches with a slatted backrest that made contact with our body in the middle of our back. We had seat belts that would keep us from being thrown out into the floor.

When we reached the foothills we began to see tighter turns one after another, and then they turned into steep switchbacks. The farther we went the steeper the switchbacks, untill we had to drive straight into the curve and back up in order to get around the switchback. Looking back down the mountain at all the switchbacks it looked almost impossible to drive a truck up the mountain. After many more switchbacks the truck pulled up on top of the mountain and stopped for a break, and to stretch our legs. I needed that, I could hardly walk when I put my feet on the ground. Someone had an altimeter and told us the altitude was 11,000 feet. You could see forever from up there. After a short break we climbed back on the truck, got belted in, and we were off again. We had a few switchbacks going down the other side of the mountain, but nothing like we had coming up.

After a few more hours of being beaten on the back by that backrest we reached our destination. The welcome committee showed us to our quarters, took us to the mess hall, got us fed, and told us when the mess hall would be open the next morning. We walked back to the barracks, got us a shower, and settled in for the night. We were all worn out from riding all day with that backrest beating us in the back. When we got up the next morning we all felt better, but we had a sore back. After walking around a bit it began to feel better. They informed us that there were two different Chinese Army`s in the area. When you step outside the barracks. Stop and look around. You will see rifle barrels aimed in your direction, but pay no attention to them. They are aimed at each other. They are waiting for the Americans` to move out. Then they will fight each other for what is left. The spoils go to the winner. We went along with what we had been told, but it was a little deffieult to step out the door and go where you wanted to go with those rifles pointed in our direction, but we got used to it in a few days. We were allowed to go to Kunming one time while we were there. I enjoyed the oriental architecture. Charles and I rode in one of those rickshaws. I felt a little guilty about riding along enjoying myself while another human being was running himself to death so we could ride.

We only spent a couple of weeks there, and early one morning we joined another group of soldiers on a C 54 four engine troop carrier headed for Karachi Pakistan. The flight was an eight hour trip. About four hours into the flight the copilot came back into the passenger area, and told us that the Tasman hall was up ahead, and the pilot was going to circle around it to the left and to the right, so we all could get a good look at it. I have never seen anything with such grandeur in my life. It looked just like I had heard it would. The plane leveled out and got back on its course toward Karachi. We all settled back in our seats for the remainder of the flight. Seven hours and fifteen minutes into the flight one of the outboard engines began to sputter. The plot tried to get it running again, but was unable to do so. He turned the switch off of that engine and made adjustments to the controls to fly with only three engines.

Everybody breathed a sigh of relief and settled back again. Twenty minutes later the other outboard engine started to sputter and the pilot could not bring it back to life. He turned the switch off on that engine also. We all knew that it was doubtful that the plane could fly very far on two engines with the passenger load. The copilot came back and told us to prepare for a crash landing. He told us that we were twenty minutes from the airport, and already had contact with the air control, and had asked for a straight in approach. We all bent over, put our head between our knees, and put our chutes between us and the front of the plane, and prayed. The pilot set the approach angle that should reach the runway before it lost all altitude, and left the rest up to the lord. As the minutes slowly dragged by we would peek out the window to see if we could see anything. After what seemed like an eternity we could see the tops of the desert bushes, but we still didn't know how far we were from the runway.

Then the landing gear made contact with the runway, and we let out a big yell. About half way down the taxi strip the plane ran out of fuel. A few seconds after we landed I felt as though I had been holding my breath for too long. It took me a while to get enough air back into my lungs. My mind kept going back in time while we were still on the plane, and I kept trying to remember how I felt when we were told that we might crash. It was all mixed up and I couldn't bring it back to mind. I do know one thing, I was never so scared in my life before or after. The plane was towed up to the tarmac and where we could walk down the steps and get our feet on the ground. It felt so good to walk around after what we had been through. It took us a while to get the incident out of our minds and be able to think about something more pleasant.

Chapter 14

We were assigned to a tent in a tent area for our quarters and told to get used to the place because we might be there for a while. Charles and I began to check out the city of Karachi The thing that impressed me most was the type of architecture used on the buildings. Everywhere we went you would see classical, colonial, and European styled buildings lining the thoroughfares. In comparison, Karachi looked similar to some of the older cities in the united states of America.

The weather there was cool, but not cold, with a breeze blowing from the Arabian sea. Christmas came and we were still there. As usual we had canned turkey with all the dressings for Christmas dinner. After eating that big meal we played games like touch football and other running games to work off the full stomach. Things were going well untill darkness. Then suddenly I got a cramping in my stomach. The latrine was located at the far side of the tent area. I hurried over to the latrine, only to find a line of soldiers holding their stomach. The latrine was like all other military latrines, it had twelve seats, which usually is adequate, but not this time. I finally had my turn in the latrine and started back to my tent. As I walked along the graveled walkway, there was men sitting on either side of the of the walk, because there was no seat in the inn. When you gotta go you gotta go. We spent the next two days cleaning up the tent area.

Uncle Sam came up with a proposition. If we would sigh up for one more year of service we would get a ninety- day re-enlistment furlough, and get to go home right away. Charles and I discussed the offer and decided to accept the offer. We went to the orderly room and signed up to serve another year. Within a week we were aboard the U. S. S. Santa Rosa, a luxury liner that had been converted into a troop carrier headed for the united states. There were five thousand of us altogether. The Santa Rosa was a beautiful ship with a lot of the amenities remaining after the conversion. The sleeping quarters were below, just above the water line. The ship was fastened together with rivets. We could hear the squeaking sound of them rubbing against the rivet holes as the ship moved through the waves. The dining area was a large room on the deck level with rows of tall tables that you could stand up and eat off of. The tables had a strip of wood along the sides and ends that extended high enough above the surface to keep the trays from sliding off the table. In rough seas you could appreciate those sideboards. But you still had to hold on to your tray or somebody else would be eating out of your tray.

When the Santa Rosa left the port of Karachi it took a southwest heading through the Arabian sea, and turned west and kept this coarse through the gulf of Aden and turned north and traveled up the red sea with Saudi Arabia on our right and Africa on our left. At the north end of the red sea the ship entered the Suez canal. After moving through the canal the ship laid over untill the next morning at port Said Egypt. We left there early the next morning and headed north northwest through the Mediterranean sea, and maintained that heading all the way through the strait of Gibraltar into the Atlantic ocean and changed our course toward the united states. The entire voyage was supposed to take twenty days and we had used up about fifteen days of that time. We were getting closer to the united stated every day, and the thought of it brought a since of excitement. We began to count the days sixteen – seventeen – eighteen – nineteen – and wouldn`t you know it. Twenty four hours from New York city we ran into the [roughest storm you could imagine.]

The waves were coming over the top of the ship. We couldn`t stand up in the corridors without hanging on to the handrail. The dining room was a mess. We couldn`t eat at the tables because we couldn`t hold on to the table and the tray at the same time and also eat. We didn`t have enough hands. We sat down against the wall and rode out the storm. I remember thinking. Here I am only twenty hours from home and I`m not going to make it. In my own awkward way I asked god to help us. I believe he did because the storm began to letup. After twenty four hours we were no closer to New York than we were before the storm. With good weather and one more day we made it to New York. We walked down the gang plank and breathed a sigh of relief. Someone with the Armed services was there to take our group to the train station and put us on a train that would take us to our respective camp, where we would be given our ninety day furlough.

Chapter 15

Charles and I was sent to Jefferson barracks mo, and was given our ninety day furlough. We were to report to Barksdale field Army Air force base at the end of our furlough. With our furlough papers in our hand, we shook hands, said goodbye. And boarded a train for our respective homes. Charles went to Springfield Mo, and I went to Bryant Arkansas. It was good to get back home. It had been twenty months since I had had seen Mama and Papa, and my brothers and sisters. My brother Dale had grown from a shy sixteen year old to a talkative young man. Lois and Hazel were almost grown. And then there was my youngest brother James. He was ten years old now, and a good looking young boy. I spent several days just visiting with the family and friends. Then I started looking for a car. I found a thirty six Plymouth on east Broadway in North Little Rock that looked good, and bought it for 600 dollars.

One afternoon I parked my Plymouth in front of Gene Rolland's store and raised the hood to check the oil, and when I did I saw a girl walking by with the most beautiful auburn hair I had ever seen. I couldn`t take my eyes off of her. She was about five feet seven or eight inches tall and about the right weight for her height. I stood there and watched her untill she went out of sight over the overpass. A day or two later I was at my sister Ruby's, house when the same girl walked by. I asked Ruby,.. Who is that girl? She said; her name is Lela Bell. She lives up the street there a little ways…" Later I described her to a friend of mine and he told me that he knew Lela Bell. I sure would like to meet her said; If you will be at the ball game at Bauxite Friday night I will introduce you to her. That sounds like a winner to me I said; When we entered the gym that night he said follow me and I will show you a good place to sit. After we were seated he told me the players usually come up here when they have a break. When they do I will introduce you to her. At half time the players didn`t come up to where we were seated. Then a little later the lights went out. The emergency lights came on but you couldn`t see a a great deal. She and some other girls came up close to where we were sitting, and I waited for him to introduce me, but he didn`t.

I thought this is the only chance I will get. I walked over to her and said; are you Lela Bell ? she said yes. I said I am Ray Graddy . she said; Hello ray I have heard a lot about you. I asked her if we could sit down and talk. We talked a few minutes and I asked if she had a ride home .She said she did. Before she could say more, I said; can I take you home? She said maybe, let me tell the coach that I have a ride home. That sounded like music to my ears. When the ball game was over we walked out to my car, got in and sat down and started talking. We talked for an hour without stopping. I drove her home and we talked untill the front door opened and she said that is my dad. That is his way of saying time to come in the house. We said good night and I asked if I could see her tomorrow. Yes you may she said I will meet you at my sister in laws house. She lives next door to your sister.

When I met Lela the next afternoon at her sister in laws house. She introduced me to her sister in law. She was a very nice looking woman with dark hair and dark complexion. She had a little girl about four and a little boy about two. The little girl walked up to me, looked me in the eye, and stomped one of my feet. Her mother said; Pat Bell you know better than that. You go to your room an don`t come out untill I tell you. She apologized to me for what the little girl had done, and I said; it`s alright it didn`t hurt much. I decided that we better go before Pat came back and stomped the other foot. I have had a lot of fun kidding Pat about that over the years.

Lela and I went to a restaurant and got something to eat and went to a movie at Bauxite After the movie we got something to drink and drove around for a while then parked and talked untill it was time to go home. When we got to her house we talked untill her daddy opened the front door which meant it is time to send that boy hone and come on in the house. We wasn`t ready to quit talking yet and we pushed our luck a little more, but when the front porch light came on we knew that we had reached the limit. We said good bye and Lela went quickly into the house. We spent a good portion of almost every day together. I think we both felt the same way about spending time together. On the third date she let me kiss her good night. I was so excited when I got home I didn`t sleep for hours We kept spending all of our time together, except when she had something else she had to do. When that happened I either went out with the guys goofing around or stayed at home with the family.

My furlough time slipped away so fast, and I didn`t realize it until it was almost over. The last week went by even faster. We spent all the time we could together. There was so many things I wanted to say to her, but I wasn`t sure haw she felt about us. I had written a letter to Charles asking him to come to Bryant a little early. And we would try to get one of Lela`s friends for him and we would go to a movie or whatever. He answered the letter saying that would be fine, and he would plan on getting here the day before we had to leave. Lela, and her friend was playing in a basket ball tournament that night. After the game we went to a late movie in Benton. After the movie we got something to drink at a drug store on the block. Then slowly drove to Bryant where Lela was spending the night with her sister in law. Lela and I was quieter than usual that night, and when we kissed good night there was a feeling that neither of us wanted it end, but every good thing has to come to a end.

Chapter 16

Charles and I left the next morning in my car about eight o`clock headed for the Barksdale Field Army Air force Base at Shreveport Louisiana. We arived there about one o`clock in the afternoon, found the orderly room, and went through the check in process. We were given all the pertinent information that all newcomers get, like where is the mess hall, where is the barracks, and where is the P. X . Then they took us to the barracks and assigned us our beds that we would be sleeping in for the next few weeks, and told us to take the rest of the day off. The next morning we were told that we would be here temporally, but they would try to keep us from being bored while we were there. They made sure that we were not bored. They put us on K.P, they put us on guard duty, they put us on yard duty to clean up the entire base. That took us several days to get that job done. I didn`t plan on coming home every week, but plans don`t always come true. I didn`t know that I would miss Lela so much. Friday morning found me at the orderly room getting a week end pass.

At four o`clock sharp I got into my car and headed toward Bryant Arkansas. In those days there were no freeways. We had to travel on two lane roads. The speed limit was sixty miles per hour. We had a lot of small towns to go through. Most of them had speed limits of twenty five miles per hour and some of them had stop lights. If you was lucky you might catch the light green. I caught some green lights and got home by eight o`clock, and went straight to Lela`s house. Lela met me at the door, and we went inside long enough to say hello to Mr. & Mrs Bell and then went over to Papa & Mama`s house because they didn`t know I was coming home that week end. We talked to them a few minutes and went driving around. I asked her if there was any place she would like to go, and she said, anywhere as long as I am with you. I assured her that I felt the same way. We drove over to Bauxite and parked in front of the Theatre and talked about what we would do Saturday and Sunday. We decided to do whatever came to mind at the time. She suggested that I come to her house about noon and have lunch with me and mom and Dad. Do you think that would be alright with them I asked?

She said; of course it will. When we got to her house we talked a few minutes, kissed good night. She went into the house and I went home to spend a little time my folks before bedtime. The next morning I stayed around the house and visited with the family until eleven o'clock, then I drove up to Lela's house and had lunch with her and her family. We stayed there for a while to let us all get a little more acquainted. Then we went to Benton and drove around the block, found a parking place, and set there watching people walk around the block. That may not sound very exciting, but that is what people would do on Saturday afternoon in Benton. Of course we talked a lot also. We didn't seem to have a problem of having something to talk about. I enjoyed talking to her. I still do. Sometimes even now we sit and talk for ever so long when we should be doing something else.

I took her home long enough change clothes and freshen up a bit, and picked her up, and went back to Benton to the movies. When I took her home we talked as long as her daddy would allow. I asked her what she was doing Sunday, and she said she needed to do some things in the house, and do some studying for tests that she had coning up. She suggested that I spend time with my family until I had to start back to camp. I really wanted to spend more time with her, but I knew she was right. As I drove back to the airbase Sunday afternoon my mind was busy thinking about all the things that had been happening in the past few weeks. Since I had met Lela my whole world had changed. If you had asked me a month ago if I had any plans to get married I would have said; no way, but after spending so much time with Lela I began to think that it might be a good idea.

I wrote Lela a letter early in the week telling her how I much missed her, and I wouldn't be coming home that week end. I stayed on base all week end, and did nothing more than eat sleep, and miss Lela. I wrote her a letter Monday telling her that I would definitely be home the next week end. Later in the week they told Charles and me that we would be transferred to Fort Totten New York within the next week. The remainder of the week went by very slowly. I thought it would never pass. I got another week end pass, and at four o`clock sharp Friday I headed to Bryant Arkansas to see Lela for another week end. I hoped she wanted to see me as much as I wanted to see her, because I had something to discuss with her that would surprise her very much. I arrived at her house at about the same time I did two weeks ago, and visited with her mom and dad a few minutes, and we went down to see my family. After visiting with them a while I took her home. We talked about what we would do the next day. When the front door opened she got out of the car and went into the house, and I went home. I spent the next morning with my family, and went to Lela`s house in time for lunch. After lunch we went to Benton for some things that Lela needed. When we got back I let her out of the car, and went back home to spend more time with my family. I knew that I would be going to new York next week, but I had not told them yet.

Lela and I went to Benton that night with the intention of going to a movie, but we found a parking space, and sat in the car talking instead. Then I drove out # 5 highway toward Little Rock. We heard thunder, and saw lighting in the west that seemed to be heading in our direction. Lela mentioned that she was scared of storms, and suggested that we go home, but that did not agree with my plans. I turned off on the road that went to Bryant, turned off into a small parking area, and said; I have something to say to you before we go home. With the wind blowing from the thunder clouds in the west, that was getting closer by the minute, I said; I know we haven`t known each other very long, but I am in love with you, and I want you to be my wife.[WILL YOU MARRY ME.]She said; yes I will. We hugged and kissed each other longer than we ever had before. Then we came back to reality. Lela asked me when do you want to get married? I said; next week. She said; how can we get married next week with you in Louisiana and me here in Arkansas? I said ;there is something I haven`t told you yet. They are sending me to Fort Totten New York next week. I have asked for a delay in route pass that will allow me to come home next Thursday. We can get married Friday, and we can have the week end together. Then I can go on up to New York on Monday. Once I am there I will start making arrangements to get you up there with me. We got out of the car and stood there with the wind blowing so hard we could hardly keep our balance, but we didn`t care. We had each other and that was all that mattered. We hugged each other tightly and enjoyed the moment. We have gone back in memory, many times, to the place where it all started.

We agreed not to tell anyone about what we were about to do, because we feared that Mister Bell would try to stop us, and we did not want that to happen. I saw Lela on Sunday morning a little while, and told her that I needed to spend more time with my family before I left to go back to Louisiana. Before I left for Louisiana Sunday afternoon I told Papa and Mama that I was being sent to Fort Totten New York, and Lela and I were getting married the next Friday before I go up there. You are not to tell anyone about this until Lela and I tell her mom and dad after the wedding. I will come back Thursday in time go to Benton to get the license. One of you will need to go with me to give me permission to get married. In fourteen days I would turn twenty one. I had been around the world, and traveled in four continents, and I still had to get permission to get married.

Chapter 17

I could hardly wait for Thursday to come so I could come back home, and get on with the plan. Mom went with me to get the license. She told me that she had told Lela about me, and had picked her out for me long before I ever laid eyes on her. That was nice of her. I thought I had picked her out all by myself. Lela had started staying with her sister in law Lucille that week, and that is where I found her Friday morning. When I knocked on the door Lela opened it and invited me in. I gave her a quick hug and kiss and sat down in a chair that she pointed out. Lucille came into the room and said hello to me and sat down to talk. Then pat came into the room, and walked over to where I was sitting, looked me in the eye and said; I`m sorry I stomped your foot before. I said; that`s ok, can we be friends? She said; yes we can, and climbed up into my lap. And we have been buddies from that day on.

About two o`clock Lela and I went to a pastors house in Bauxite and asked him if he would perform the wedding ceremony for us. First he tried to talk us out of it, but we said; we loved each other, and we want to be married. He had his wife to be the witness, and went on with the ceremony. We said our I do`s and when he said; you may kiss the bride. We kissed briefly, thanked him and went on our way. Then we went to her mom and dads house and told them that we were married an hour ago. They didn`t like it much, but we expected that. Her dad said something like, I aught to whip both of you, but I don`t think he meant that.Lela was graduating from high school that night. When we arived at the school house she told a friend about it, and the news moved through the crowd like a fire through a wheat field. When the graduating exercises were over we tried to get to the car as quickly as possible, but the pranksters were ahead of us. they had decorated the car, tin cans and all.

When we left the school house there was a convoy following us with horns blowing, whopping and hollowing, and all the trimmings.

We headed toward Little Rock and finallly lost them. We didn`t mind them following us. we might have been disappointed if they hadn`t. We found a nice motel on Asher avenue with separate cabins and rented it for two nights. After staying there two nights we went back to Lela`s parents house, and visited with them for a while. Then we went to Lucilles` house where Lela changed her clothes, and got ready to take me to the railroad station to board the train for new York City. Getting on that train was the hardest thing I ever had to do. We had only been married two days, and I was leaving her behind. It didn`t seem fair, but I was a soldier, and I had to do what I was told.

The train pulled into grand central station around noon the next day. I got off the train, set my duffle bag down, and did a three sixty to see what was inside the station. I could hardly believe it. That was the biggest building I have ever seen under one roof. I believe you could put the city of Benton inside the station and had room to spare. They had big stores, hotels, and restaurant inside the station. You could live there without ever going outside, if you had the money of course. I asked a person at a ticket counter how to get to fort Totten. He told me that I would need to take the subway and get off at the main street station. I asked him where I could buy a ticket, and he said right here. He handed me a ticket I paid him for it, and he pointed at an opening, and said; go through that opening and take the stairs down to the subway platform, and get on the train when it stops. The train stayed underground for a long time. Then it emerged from the tunnel, and moved along through areas that had small stores, service stations, and residential buildings. Then it went underground again. I began to think that I had missed the main street station. I asked the train conductor when we would get to the main street station. He said ; it is the next one. I got off at the next stop, walked up the stairs, and would you believe it, there was the bus station. I purchased a ticket, and got on the bus for fort Totten.

We traveled several miles, and turned off onto a highway that seemed to be leading out onto an island. After a few more miles we arived at fort Totten. The bus driver gave me directions to the adjutants office. I went to the office, and checked in. The officer had an assistant to show me to my barracks, and assign me a bed. I found the bed number that he assigned to me, and started to put my clothes away when I heard someone call my name and turned to see who it was. It was Charles Pate. He got there before I did, and there was only two beds between us. he said; well did you get married. I said; I sure did. He then admitted that he was married before we went to Louisiana. I said; you rascal. You let me get you a date with Lela`s best friend, and you didn`t tell me that you were married. I don`t know what to think about you. I can`t believe you would do that. He said; no harm done. I was a perfect gentleman with her. Maybe you were, but that was a lousy thing to do.

Chapter 18

A fort at Willets point on long island sound was officially designated Camp Morgan in 1861, after Govenor Edwin D Morgan of New York. In 1898 Camp Morgan was re-named after Major Joseph Totten. In 1944: Fort Totten became headquarters of the north Atlantic region of the Air Transport Command. My Branch of Service. In 2005 Fort Totten park was opened to the public. I didn`t stay there long until they transferred Charles and me to Mitchell Field Air Force Base on T. D. Y. [Temporary Duty.] which was six miles north of Hempstead N. Y. My duty there was to service and maintain all A. T. C. aircraft. In less than a month after we were married I received a phone call from Mama telling me that Lela an attack of appendicitis, and had taken her to Dr. Rogers hospital in Searcy Arkansas for surgery. I arranged for an emergency furlough with the adjutants office, and caught a train for Searcy Arkansas. It took me something like eighteen hours to get there, and by that time the surgery had already been done. When I walked into the hospital room she was sitting up in bed as though nothing was wrong with her. Of course she was sore for several days. As soon as Dr. Rogers discharged her from the Hospital, I got Gene Rolland to come to Searcy, and take her home. He had a big easy riding car that she could lie down in, and she rested easy all the way home. I tried to pay Gene for the trip, but he said; no way. You are in service to protect our country, and that is the least I can do for a soldier.

I stayed home long enough to make sure that Lela would be alright, and caught a train back to Mitchell field air force base N.Y. It didn`t take long to find out that I could not afford to bring Lela up there with me. I began to go home as often as possible. The base had a few flight officers that wee required to fly a certain amount of hours each month in order to receive flight pay, they would check out an airplane Friday afternoon, and fly to Little Rock Arkansas or Dallas Texas or Memphis Tennessee. We could get a week end pass, sign on as a crewman, and that made it legal. If they flew to Little rock I had it made. Benton was only twenty miles away. If they flew to Dallas, and landed at Little Rock I had it made. If they flew to Memphis only, I had to board a plane that was headed for Dallas, and landed at Memphis. The first time I did this I got off the airplane there, and started hitch hiking home. Most of the people were going the wrong direction, but eventually someone came along that was going the right direction

A man and his son picked me up, and took me to Lonoke Arkansas. I didn`t wait long before a man stopped, and said; where are you going I said; Benton Arkansas. He; said get In. I`m going to north little rock, and I`m going right by the bus station. You can a catch a bus to Benton there. It is too late in the night to hitch hike. He drove back onto the highway, and speeded up at a pace that I wasn`t used to, and when he came to the first curve I realized I was in for the ride of my life. I got a good hold of the seat, and held on the best I could. He drove that twenty five miles in twenty minutes or less on a two lane crocked road . When he let me off at the station I thanked him for the ride, and thanked the lord for keeping me safe. I went into the bus station and bought a ticket to Benton Arkansas, got on the bus, sat back, relaxed, and tried to get over that wild ride. Then pushed the button to get off at the road to Bryant I walked the two miles home.

I enjoyed the remainder of Friday night Saturday, and Saturday night with my wife. I had to catch the plane in Memphis at two o`clock Sunday afternoon, I borrowed my brothers oldsmobile to drive to Memphis. My wife and her Brother went with me , and they were going to drive the car back to Benton. Everything went well until we got to Brinkley. A tire blew out on the car, and we could not buy a tire on Sunday. We had to get a motel room, stay there for the night, and buy a tire Monday morning. We got up early Monday morning, ate breakfast, bought a tire, had it mounted, rolled it back to the car, and put it back on the wheel. We got in the car and headed for Memphis. There is one thing that I didn`t tell you about the old car. The engine would stop running every time you stopped. My wife had to reach down and push on the gas petal to keep it running. We had a lot of trouble getting though all the stop lights in Memphis, before we got to the airport. I went into the military section of the airport, and inquired about a flight to New York. I was told that there was no flights scheduled for New York, but there was a flight going to Washington D. C. at eight o`clock that night. I went back out to the car and told my wife that I had a flight to Washington D. C., and they could go on back home.

I walked around inside of the airport, killing time until it was time for my flight to leave for Washington. I slept most of the way there. Then I got off the plane, and waited some more. The next morning I realized I was short on money. I didn`t know I would spend so much getting back to home base. I asked some one if there was a western union nearby, and was told that there was one up on the hill outside the base. I walked over to the gate, and caught a bus up to the Western Union office. I sent a message to my wife telling her that I needed a certain amount of money. They told me to come back in three hours, and it would be there. I went back inside the base and waited three hours, went back to Western union, picked up my money, and went back through the gate to the waiting room where I waited for my flight to New York. After landing at Mitchell Field N.Y. I went to my barracks, and slept the rest of the night. When I got to work Wednesday morning I was two days late getting back to the base. As I walked into the building I met the officer that issued my weekend pass. He said, good morning, glad to see you back. I said, I guess you know I`m two days late! He said, no you`re not late! Your plane developed engine trouble near Nashville, and landed there for repairs. They are waiting for parts to fix it with. You are not late until the plane gets back to home base. That was an unexpected relief.

Chapter 19

My stay at Mitchell field was about ten months. I went into new York several times wile I was there. The transportation that went into the city always took us to Penn station. Sometimes I would walk over to Grand Central station just to walk around, and see all the things that was within the station. I never failed to be amazed at the size of it. I attended two or three stage shows there but I can`t remember the names of any of them. If I wanted to go eat at a restaurant, or see a movie I would catch a bus into Hempstead which was only six miles from the base.

I didn`t buddy around with Charles much after he told me that he got married during his reenlistment furlough. We were still friends, but we didn`t go anywhere together. He went his way and I went mine. On the week ends that I didn`t go home I would stay around the barracks and read or play cards with other guys that stayed on base. Most of them would sleep until noon on Saturday and Sunday. But I liked to eat. I got up early both mornings and went to the mess hall and ate a good breakfast. I might go back to the barracks and then sleep to noon, but it was on a full stomach.

After being at Mitchell field for a few months I received a request to report to Fort Totten to receive a Corporals rating. I thought, it`s about time, but I reported to fort Totten as I had been requested, and let them pin the corporals stripes on my sleeve. It did increase my pay a little. It also increased my responsibility. At that point in time I was doing what ever I had to do until it came time for me to be discharged. I had been in service two years and eight months. All I wanted to do now was to show up each day, do what there was to do, go back to the barracks, and sleep all night. Then show up again the next day and do the same thing over again until the day came for me to go home and be a husband to my wife, and be happy for ever and ever, and ever A-men.

The time moved so slowly, month after month untill one day I was notified that I should report to Fort Totten to go through the process of being discharged. That was the day I had been waiting for. I hurried over to Headquarters, and told them that I was there to get my discharge. I was sent from one office to another to get a form signed by each office. When I got to the Adjutants office he looked at the form, and said; you was promoted to corporal only a short time ago. If I had known that I would not have given it to you. I said; sir. I was kept waiting for three years because all ratings were frozen. I believe I deserved this one. I signed the form, handed it back to me, and said; good luck. I said; thank you sir, and left his office with the discharge in my hand. The date on my discharge was march 24/1947.

I went back to Mitchell field, packed all of my belongings in my duffel bag, and went over to the orderly room to wait for a bus to Hempstead. While I was waiting the adjutant came by and saw me in the waiting area. He walked over to me, and asked me where I was going. I told him I was going home. He said; you can't do that. We need you here. He sat down and started telling me all the good things he would do for me. He told me he would see to it that I was promoted to staff Sergeant in a matter of days, and promoted to Tech Sergeant within four Months. I said Captain I know you mean well, but I have done a Tech Sergeants work for two years for P. f. C. pay, and I don't want to wait any more. I want to go home, get a job that will pay me what I'm worth, and see if I can make it in Civilian life. He said; I understand, good luck to you. I rode the bus to town, and boarded the train for Little rock Arkansas.

When I arived in Little Rock I got off the train, found a phone and called Gene Rollands store and asked him to get word to Dale that I will be getting off the bus at highway 5 and Bryant road, and I need him to pick me up there. When I got of the bus, Dale was there waiting for me. He took me to where Lela was living in an apartment in Pine heaven. It was so good to be home. We had not spent much time together since we were married, but we had spent enough time together for her to be pregnant, and she looked like she might be about ready, but according to the count it would be another month. We were so happy to see each other we talked until late in the night. After breakfast the next morning we drove over to see my family for a while, and then went and visited her folks.

After a week at home I decided I needed to look for a job. My mustering out pay would not last very long. Reynolds Mining Co was only one mile across the highway from where we lived. I went there and told them I was raised on a farm in Van Buren County ark, and I had just recently been discharged from the Army Air Force. I told them I was looking for a job. They asked me where I was from. I told them I was from Bryant, but I was raised in Van Buren County. He told me to come back Monday morning, and they would get me signed up. When I got there Monday they had me to fill out forms giving them my complete history, and told me to come back Tuesday to go to work. When I got there Tuesday they told me they would start me out in the labor pool, and I could work up from there. When I got to the labor pool I ran into a guy by the name of Oscar " Buddy" Rolland. He told me that was his first day there also. We worked some together at different times.

They had us doing a little of everything. We cleaned out drainage ditches, trash cans, and kilns that needed fire brick replaced that had fallen out. I witnessed an accident one day that I could not forget. A man fell twenty feet off of a steel beam to a concrete floor, landing on his head and shoulders. It was a horrible sight to see. The sound of the safety horns echoing off the tanks and building, mixed with the screaming of the siren as the ambulance moved in to pick up the injured man, and take him to the Hospital. It left me with a strange feeling of uneasiness. It was a feeling I could not shake. I felt as though I was fenced in with no way out. The feeling kept coming back again, and again to the point that I decided I could not work there any more. I told my Boss I was leaving at the end of the week. He asked me why I was leaving, and I told him I wanted to look for some other type of work. In the midst of all this our first daughter was born on April 23 rd 1947 ; and we named her Constance Diane Graddy. That was only a month after I was discharged from the Army Air Force. I needed a job that would pay more.

My Brother Ralph suggested that I consider learning to become a carpenter. He had learned the trade in an N.Y.A. program at south side High School while he was a teenager. I took his advice, went to Little

Rock , and got a job with a contractor that was building small houses near the airport that sold for five, and six thousand dollars each. There was a lot of ex service men and their wives that could afford a house that size, and they were being sold as fast as we could build them. I worked there until all of the lots were built on. Then I worked for him on another project near fair park Boulevard, and twelfth street. The houses we built there were larger, and a bit more expensive. When I first went to work for this contractor I talked to him about the on the job training program. This program would allow him to pay me less per hour, and as a Veteran I could draw $90:00 per month for going to school at nights to learn plan reading as well as learning to read a framing square which was the carpenters Bible. Soon after I went to work him his foreman began letting me do the outside trim. After he found out that I could do the trim outside he started having me do the inside trim as well. I kept on doing everything he put me on to the best of my ability, and he kept giving me more important things to do.

By this time I felt that I had learned enough to build my own house. I took off about two & a half weeks, and Papa, Dale, and myself went up to the old home place, and stayed in the old house while we cut all the pine timber on the place, had it hauled to the sawmill, and made into lumber. I might add that it rained one night, and we got wringing wet. Papa sold all the lumber except what dale, and I needed to frame a house for each of us. In the meantime I had purchased a lot, built a garage on it, and put a wood floor in it. I also put partitions in it so we could live in it until we got the house built. At this point I had done just about everything there was to do on a house except build a foundation, but I had watched the bricklayers lay brick, and I thought if they can do it. I can do it. As I walked around over the lot to get an idea where to put the house a man came along, and asked what are you going to do there? I said. I`m going to build a house. Where are you going to put it? I said; I don`t know. What kind of a house he asked? I said; I don`t know. He said; do you know how to build a house?  I said; no I don`t. He said; if you don`t know where to put it, and you don`t know what kind it is, and you know how to build a house. How are you ever going to get it built? I said, well I thought, if I stood around here long enough somebody would come along, and tell me how to do it.

I staked out the house, and started digging the footing, and sure enough somebody came by and offered his suggestions on how to dig a footing. I said; thank you sir, and kept on digging. I rented a concrete mixer and poured the footing, but nobody offered any suggestions on how to do that. I must have been doing it right. I started laying the brick foundation and another fellow came by, and gave me his ideas on how to lay brick. I started putting the floor joist in, and a another fellow told me how he always put in the floor joist. I then started cutting the wall studs to frame the walls, and you guessed it, a guy told me how he always framed the walls, and the roof. I thanked him for his advise also. With the advice of the good hearted men in the neighborhood I got the house framed up with the roofing, and siding installed. I did have one man to help me. Dale helped me all the way. Then we moved inside, hung, and finished the sheetrock. Installed the doors, and the interior trim, and moved into the house. There were a few things remaining to do, but I could do them later. I had also promised Dale that I would help him build his house, as pay back for him helping me, and I did start doing that a few weeks later. I also made application for a job with the Postal department, and was told that they were not hiring anyone right now, but they gave me a study manual to read that would help me to be more qualified when they did call me to report for a job

When Diane was almost a year old Lela and I decided we should start taking her to church. The first Sunday, we went to the Methodist church, and we enjoyed it very much. The following Sunday, we went to the Missionary Baptist church across the highway, and we liked it even better. We kept attending church there as long as we lived in Bryant. Later in the year, during a revival meeting we both accepted Christ as our personal savior, and were baptized in one of the Bauxite pits, and became a members of the Baptist church in Bryant.

At this point in time I got the opportunity to go to work for Fred Parrott, the contractor that Ralph was working for. Fred agreed to hire me if I would join the Carpenters Union ,and start as a third year apprentice. I went to the Union Hall and took a verbal test. The Union Officials suggested that I join as a full joiner Carpenter, but I told them I wanted to learn what a joiner Carpenter was supposed to know, before I joined as a full joiner carpenter, I only had an agreement with

Fred for a third year apprentice. With that done I told the contractor I had been working for that I would be leaving at the end of the week.

The best I can remember I started working for Fred in mid-year of 1948: Ralph had told Fred what kind of work I could do, and he put me to doing inside trim right away, and soon had me building cabinets. These houses were much larger than I had been working on, and had a lot more cabinets in them. In those days there was no such thing as pre-built cabinets. We built them in-place one piece at a time. When the house was framed up with the outside wall sheathing installed, and roofing was complete. What we called dried in. We would move inside, and start trimming out and building the cabinets. It took a long tine to trim out, and build all the cabinets in a house. I worked on a lot of houses on the streets over looking the Arkansas river while I was working for Fred. Some of these houses were not the run of the mill straight roofed houses. The floor plan on these houses were so cut up that it was difficult to do the roof framing. Once in a while I would have the opportunity to go out and work with the framing crew, and learn how to fame those defficult roofs. I learned there was a lot more to framing a roof than most of us realize. A good framing carpenter is worth his weight in gold.

Chapter 20

Among the many friends we made after joining the Baptist Church was Harold and Fern Sullivan. One Sunday they invited us to their home for dinner after church. When we had finished eating they asked us if we would like to take a drive over to the airport and watch the airplanes for a while. We said; that would be fun. On the way over there Harold told us that he had been taking flying lessons, and he was enjoying them very much. After watching the planes for a while, Harold said ; come with me. I will introduce you to the man who owns these airplanes, and runs the flight training program. We found Mr. Brewer around at the end of the hanger, visually inspecting the outside of the plane for surface defects. Harold said; Lewis, this is Ray Graddy, Ray meet Lewis Brewer. We said our hello`s, and he began telling me about the plane, and asked if I had ever been up in one, I said; Yes I have. My first ride was in a C 46 cargo plane over the Himalayan mountains between India, and China. Did you enjoy it ? I said; I sure did. Would you like to take a ride in this one? I said, "yes." He said, "get in."

I got in buckled my seat belt, and he taxied around to the end of the runway, checked out the engine, and took off down the runway. He climbed up to five hundred feet, flew around over the city, and showed me some of the places of interest. Then he climbed up to a thousand feet, leveled off, and ask if I would like to take the controls, and try my hand at flying the plane. I said; sure I would kike that. I put my feet and hands on the controls, and he told me it`s all yours. He instructed me how to make a left turn and a right turn, and how to bring it back to level. Then he took over the controls, circled the field and landed. As we got out of the plane he asked if I would like to take flight lessons? I said; yes I think I would. He said come on inside, and I will get you signed up on the G.I. Bill, and it want cost you anything. Then he told me when to come back to get started.

I went to the airport Tuesday afternoon for my first lesson, and met my instructor Dean Carter . Dean had been a bomber pilot in service, and had nerves of steel. He would let you go to the point of danger before he would take over the controls. He would explain how to do a maneuver, and let you do it then tell you what you did wrong. He told me up front that the art of flying was being able to coordinate the foot controls with the hand controls. It is that simple. When I had about five and a half hours in flight time we landed, and dean said, you are doing fine. I think you are ready to solo. Lets take a break, get something to drink , and we will go back up, circle the field, and if you do alright on the landing, I will get out and you can go back up, and do your solo flight. That scared me out of my wits. When we went back up I couldn`t do anything right. We landed, and he told me to come back in a couple of days. I shouldn`t have told you that you could solo after the break, that gave you too much time to think about it.

I met Dean at the airport Thursday afternoon and we went up, flew around a few minutes, made a couple of take off, and landings, Dean got out of the plane without a warning and said; time to solo. Closed the door and walked away. Without hesitation I taxied out to end of the runway, turned out on the runway opened the throttle, and took off down the runway, and eased the plane off the ground, and I was airborne. It was no trouble at all. I flew around over town, entered the flight pattern, made a couple of take off and landings, taxied up to the hanger, turned off the ignition, got out of the plane, and proudly walked over to the hanger while everyone was cheering for me, and saying we knew you could do it. Dean walked over to me, stuck out his hand, and said; congratulations, I knew you were ready, but you needed to know that you were ready.

After soloing I started working toward getting my private license. In addition to having to have at least forty two hours flight time, I had to study, and pass a test on map reading, and meteorology. I also had to make one cross country flight with landings at Stutgard, Conway , and back home to Benton with an instructor, and one solo flight in the opposite direction. When we got to Stutgard on the first cross country flight I circled the field, and was on the final approach when Dean said; let me have the controls. He said; it`s so far to the hanger I will show you how to get there quicker. He landed on the right wheel with the right wing no more than a foot off the pavement, and flew the plane in an arc to the right up close to the hanger, let the other wheel down,and taxied up to the to the hanger, and stopped. Then said; don`t try that until you have more time in the air. We got out of the plane, went inside, and got us a cold drink. We stayed a few minutes, went back to the plane got in , taxied out to the runway, and took off to Conway. We landed at Conway, taxied up to the other end of the strip, turned out on the runway and, took off for Benton I flew a couple of hours each week to get enough time to get my private license. In the meantime I took all my test. Then one day Mr. Brewer handed me my private license. Now you can take up a passenger. I turned to my wife, and said; come with me. You can be my first passenger.

When I got back from taking my wife for a ride. Mr. Brewer asked me if I wanted to start training for a commercial license? He said your G. I. Bill will pay for that also. I said, yes I believe I would. To be eligible for a commercial certificate you must hold at least a private pilot certificate. Meet the aeronautical experience requirements that apply to the aircraft category and class ratings sought, pass the knowledge test, pass the practical test, and log at least 200: hours in powered aircraft of which 50hours is of pilot in command flight time, and 50: hours as cross country flight time. You also must have a medical certificate from a Dr. certifying that you are physically able to fly an aircraft. Mr. Brewer supplied me with the study manuals to enable me to pass the test of the required subjects.

It took me the better part of two years to log enough flight time to be eligible for a commercial certificate. I would go to the airport and fly an hour two times a week. And go to the airport on Sunday afternoon, and fly an hour or so. And we would go on a cross country flight now, and then. When I went to the airport in the afternoon on week days. I spent most of my time practicing the various aeronautical maneuvers that my instructor had taught me. Sometimes I would spend a full hour practicing one maneuver. When you consider all the different maneuvers there was to learn. You could log a lot of flight time just practicing them alone. In addition to that you had to study the manuals to learn the aeronautical terms. You also had to learn the theory of flight. You had to know how each moveable surface reacted to the forces it came in contact with. Then you had to pass a test on the required subjects. Add them all up, and you will find that you have spent a lot of time, and energy to qualify for the commercial certificate. I advised Mr. Brewer that I had met all the requirements, and was ready to take the flight test.

He arranged for the time, and place with the instructor to give me the test. On the test date I went to the instructors office in Little Rock. He took me out to the plane. We walked around the plane looking for any visual defects. Got into the plane, started the engine, went through the pre-flight check, and took off for the test area. We climbed up to the proper altitude and started the test. He instructed me to do a multitude of maneuvers ending with a spin to the left, and a spin to the right. When we came out of the last spin. He said; that's good enough for me. Lets go back to the office and I will sign your certificate. After landing at the Airport we went to his office he signed my certificate, handed it to me, and said; good luck. I said; thank you, and left his office. I hurried home to tell Lela. I think she was as happy about it as I was. I took a break for a while. I guess I was a little burned out after cramming for all those tests.

Chapter 21

I had a younger sister that married a man that was born and raised in Bryant that had gone to California to work. Hazel got acquainted with Johnny Neal when he would come home now and then to visit his folks. While he was visiting them in 1950: he and hazel got married, and she went back to California with him. They came back to visit the following year, and while they were here they talked to us about coming out there, and getting t a job there. Johnny said; there was plenty work there, and I would not have any trouble getting a job. That sounded pretty good, and aside from that, Hazel, and I had always been very close. I kept thinking she might need me close by to look after her. After all she was only sixteen years old when she got married. We thought about that quite often, and in may of 1951:, we made up our minds to go. We had a lot of things to do before we could go. We sold our house, bought a new Studebaker Starlite coupe automobile, found a small potato bug looking trailer to haul our bags, bedding, and clothing, and painted it blue to match the car. We went to Senath Mo. to visit my folks before we left for California. When we got ready to come back home my mother broke down and said; I`ll never see you again, I just know it. When we got back home we visited our family there, and on the first day of June 1951, we headed for California.

We didn`t get very far the first day, I had bought a sun visor for the car and they didn`t get it installed properly, and we had to stop at a garage to get it fixed. We also had a few other things that we had to stop for, and we only got to Clinton Oklahoma the first day, but we didn`t mind. We were on a new adventure, to places we had never been before and we were having a good time. In Oklahoma City we had changed from Highway 64 to Route 66, which is also known as the Mother Road, that was traveled by the fictional Joad family in The Grapes of Wrath as they fled from the infamous Oklahoma Dust Bowl in the 1930,s, in the hope of finding a better life in California. We made better time the next day. We went from Clinton, Oklahoma, into the Texas panhandle, through Amarillo, into New Mexico, and stopped at Santa Rosa to spend the night. New Mexico was different from the states that we had been through. We had been seeing trees, bushes, and other types of foliage. But this was a more barren landscape.

We left Santa Rosa the next morning, and headed on west through Albuquerque, over the continental devide, through Gallup, and into Arizona. We had to leave Route 66 by turning to the right onto Pinta Road to visit the Petrified Forest which was very interesting. What looked like logs was as hard as nails, and the Painted Desert was a sight to behold, with a multitude of colors as far as the eye could see. Then we returned to Pinta, road and got back on Route 66, and continued our journey toward California. Arizona was, and still is Indian country. By looking off to the north as you drive along you could see the Indian cliff dwellers, They had dug caves back into the cliff, and made living quarters, with long skinny wooden ladders reaching from the floor of the cliff up to the respective cave.

When we reached Flagstaff I told Lela I wanted to keep driving because I wasn`t very tired, and I wanted to get as far as possible that day. I hadn`t driven far beyond Williams when I got so sleepy that I couldn`t keep my eyes open.  I told Lela that I couldn`t stay awake, and we had to find a place stay the night. We came to small town by the name of Sligman, and began to look for a tourist court [as they were called in those days.] The only thing we could find was a tiny Tourist court with only one room left. It wasn`t much to look at, but we didn`t have a choice. W got up the next morning and drove through Peach Springs, and started down the mountain to the lower elevation below. As we drove down the mountain we could see the landscape stretching out in front of us all the way to the horizon. When we got to Kingman we left Route 66, and took highway 93 toward Las Vegas Nevada. Lela`s uncle Todd Duval had told us not to go over Needles mountain, because its too dangerous. We took his advise. We traveled up 93 highway through Wells Nevada, and on up to Boulder Dam where we took time to look at the sights there, and went on to Las Vegas. As we drove into town we were looking for the highway that would take us to Las Angles.

We stopped at a traffic light. While we were waiting for the light to change, Diane our four year old daughter began to yell, there's uncle Johnny repeatedly, and lo and behold it was my Brother in law Johnny Neal walking across the street in front of us. By that time he recognized us, and motioned for us to turn to the right. We turned right. Found a parking place to park and visited a few minutes. He was returning to work after lunch when he heard Diane yelling his name. how often do you think that would happen? He told us if we would turn around and go through the same intersection we would be headed toward Las Angles.

We reached the outskirts of Vegas in no time at all it seemed, because it was not a big town at that point in time. The best that I can remember the population was 6,000 + or -- 500 people. The last place on the strip was the last frontier. The next place we came to was Baker California, the hottest place in the United States of America. We stopped there, took a short break, and kept driving down highway 91 to Barstow, where we got back on route 66, and travled through Victorville, San Bernardino, and on to Las Angeles. Lela and I had been taking turns driving, a little ways beyond San Bernardino it was Lela's turn to drive. I found a place to pull off the highway, she got under the wheel, pulled back onto the traffic lanes. She hadn't been driving long until the traffic got heavier. They were passing her on both sides.

She said; I can't do this. They're swishing by me on both sides, and I just can't drive in this kind of traffic. I told her to poll over on the shoulder as soon as she got a chance, and I would take it from here on. We swopped seats, and went on our way. Hazel had told me to turn off of Route 66 onto Sunset Boulevard to get to her home. We drove up Sunset street, turned right on the street she told as, and drove up in her driveway. We enjoyed the week end with Hazel and Margaret who was there also. Monday I went to the carpenter Local Union hall and asked them about work. They asked if I Had a Union card. I showed them my card. They looked at it and said; we don't have any calls for a carpenter, but if you find a job, we will give you a work order. They gave me several contractors names, and addresses to check out.

Chapter 22

I started checking each address on the list, and got the answer from each contractor. We don`t need anyone right now, but check with us later. I heard that all day long day after day. On the third day I was driving west in the afternoon. As I approached a traffic light the sun was shinning in my eyes, and I could not tell if it was green or red. I did what I thought was best, and stopped, but the man behind me didn`t. He hit me hard enough to knock me across a four lane boulevard, and half way down the next block. The impact broke the back of seat, and left me in the prone position. I had a problem getting up so I could get my foot on the to brake to stop the car. The other driver came down to see if I was hurt. I told him I didn`t think I was. But I was scared half to death. My trunk was caved in something awful. It made me sick to look at it. We exchanged insurance information. He told me how to get to his insurance Co Office, and I was able to drive my car there to get them to look at it. they told me to take it to a dealer near by to get it fixed. The dealer said it would take three days to fix it, and gave me a courtesy car to drive.

They called me when the body work on my car was completed, and I went to get it. I walked all around the car to see if they had done every thing they were supposed to do. Everything looked good. I got in, sat down, checked the seat back, and it seemed to be alright. I drove back to Hazel`s house to show Lela the Car, and spent the rest of the day looking for a job, but I didn`t have any luck. After two weeks of looking for a job, with no prospects in sight I began to feel discouraged, to say the least. Johnny came home from Vegas that weekend, and I told him that I had not had any luck at all finding a job. He suggested that we all go back to Vegas with him, Sunday afternoon and he would talk to the superintendent of the J.C . Penney project where he was installing an elevator. We all got in separate cars Sunday afternoon, and drove to Vegas, and got rooms in a tourist court. I got up Monday morning, went with Johnny to work. We went straight to the superintendents office. Johnny introduced me to him, and told him I was looking for a job as a carpenter. He asked me if I was a Joyner carpenter. I said; yes I am. He asked if I had any experience on commercial work. I said; no I haven`t, but I can do it. Just tell me what you want me to do, and I will do it. He told me to go to the local union, and get a referral.

I went to the local union, got the referral, brought it back, and gave it to him. He allowed me to work the remainder of the day. The temperature was a lot higher than I was used to, but the humidity was a lot lower. In fact the heat would dry the perspiration off as fast as it would form. I made it alright through the first week. In fact I rather enjoyed it. The following Monday when I got to the room I saw signs that Lela, and Diane had been crying. I didn`t say anything about it. .The next evening when I came in I saw the same thing as the day before. I still didn`t say anything. The same thing happened the next two days. That was all I could take. I brought up the fact that I was aware that they had been crying every day that week, and said; lets talk about it. That was all it took to start the tears flowing. They both said; we don`t like it here. We are homesick and want to go home. What to do! I told them I would take them home.

We told Johnny, and Hazel during the weekend of our decision to go back to Arkansas. Monday morning I went straight to the Superintendents office. I told him that my wife, and daughter had been crying each day when I got home, and I have to take them home to Arkansas. He said you can`t do that, I need you here. That puts me in a bind. I said, I`m terribly sorry. I know I should give you more notice, but I can`t, stand that crying any more, he said; alright, give me a little time, and I will get your money for you. He came back in about an hour, and gave me my money, and said; I wish you could have stayed with me longer. I said; I wish I could have also. I did enjoy working for you. I went by where Johnny was installing an elevator, and told him that I was going to the motel and start packing, and loading the car, and trailer. We had everything loaded when Johnny got to the motel. We had lunch together, and talked about things that might have been. I told Hazel that before we came to California, I had the feeling that she needed me nearby to sort of look after her, but since I had been here I could easily see that she could look after herself. I thanked Johnny for helping me get the job, and I was sorry that things turned out the way they did. We all hugged, cried, and told each other how good it was to be together for the time we had. We said goodbye, got into the car, and drove up to Fairmont street, turned left and drove down the street toward Kingman Arizona. As we drove down 93 highway we talked about how good it will be to get back to Arkansas. We decided it would be easier on us if we took turns driving. I told Lela that I would drive through Kingman, and on over to Williams, and then we could start swapping out every two hours.

We would stop when we got hungry, and then go as far as we could without stopping. Diane furnished the music. She stood on the hump between me, and her mother, and sang tidley winky woo. All the way home, just like she did all the way to California. I don't think I have gotten so tired of anything before, but that kept her occupied. When we got to Williams Arizona we stopped, and got something to eat. Then Lela took her first turn driving. We did alright the first few hours, but when we got over in New Mexico we began to encounter detours around strips of repair on Route 66, and it went on all through the night, and as a result neither of us got any sleep. As time went by the road seemed to get better, but when I was approaching Amarillo Texas the sun was coming up in the eastern sky, and I got so sleepy I couldn't keep my eyes open. I opened the wing glass so the air would hit me in the face. I pinched myself, slapped myself, and when all seemed hopples, I saw a restaurant up ahead. I pulled into the parking space, went in, and had breakfast. When we finished breakfast we put gas in the car, and got back on the road again with Lela driving.

We kept driving, swapping seats, and driving again as we left the panhandle, and entered Oklahoma, drove across the state, and entered Arkansas, and continued driving until we came to Ozark Arkansas where we stopped for gas. While we were there Lela said; I feel awful. I answered, so do I. she said; why don't we stay here tonight? We could get cleaned up, get a good nights sleep, and go on home in the morning looking decent instead of looking like a couple of bums with their little bum. We secured a room in a nice motel, and did exactly what she had suggested. We got up the next morning feeling refreshed, but hungry. We went across the street to a restaurant , and ate a good breakfast. When we left the motel we looked like a nice couple, and their beautiful little girl going on a well deserved vacation. We were actually coming home from an almost six weeks vacation.

As we traveled along the highway, there was a hint of excitement in all of our voices, as we talked about where we had been, and what we would do when we got home. When we got to Mr. Bells house they were surprised, because they didn`t have a telephone, and we couldn`t let them know that we were coming home. We stayed with Lela`s folks two or three days, and rented a house, up the street from where they lived, and moved into it. We stayed there about six months, and moved down the street to the Watts house. We lived there one year, and moved to a house on river street in Benton.

Chapter 23

Ralph told Fred Parrott that I was back, and he told Ralph to tell me that I could come back to work for him any time I was ready. The following Monday I went with the guys to work, and he sent me back to Nolen Blass`s house which was the same place I was working before I left. I continued working for Fred for several years, doing basically the same type of work that I had been doing. In the meantime Jimmy Mc New and I heard of a J- 3 cub for sale near Crossett. We called the guy, and talked to him about it. We asked him how much he was asking for it, and he said; three hundred, and fifty dollars. We got directions to where he lived, and drove down there the following Saturday and looked at it, We took it up, flew around a few minutes, came back, landed , and told him we would take it. .The next Saturday we went back down there, filled it up with gas, and I got in the plane, and flew it back, and landed it on Harold Sullivan's air strip behind his house, and parked it there. Harold had told us before hand, that we could keep it there. Incidentally, Jimmy drove the car back home. We cleaned it up, flew it over to Benton, and showed it to Mr. Brewer. He looked it over, and said; it looks good. You should get a lot of use out it. He asked us if we had been doing any flying. We said; not since we got our commercial license.

While we were there Mr. Brewer started talking to Jimmy and me about taking the flight Instructors course. He told us we could teach our wives, Lela and Fay, how to fly as we took the course. We told him we would think about it. Jimmy, and I sat down with our wives and asked them if they would like to learn to fly an airplane. They first said; no we don`t. But the more we discussed it the more they seemed to be in favor of it. Then one of them looked at the other and said; why not? The other said; lets do it. Jimmy and I signed up to go through the Instructors course. The first few hours that Lela and I flew together I would let her take the controls to get the feel of doing a maneuver, and bringing the plane back to a level attitude. I also let her do the same maneuvers by herself. Then I began to have her put her hands and feet on the controls to get the feel of them on take off, and landings When I felt that she was getting the hang of it I told her that she would do the next take off, and I will be there to take over the controls if necessary, but I don`t think I will have to do that.

The only thing Lela was having a problem with was landing. Her approach was very good, but she couldn`t keep the plane from bouncing when it landed, I could not detect what she was doing wrong. On the next landing. I watched her very closely on the final approach, and I noticed something that I thought might be causing the problem. I had her to taxi back up to the other end of the runway, and stop. I said; tell me where you are looking just before landing? She said; I`m looking straight over the nose of the plane. I told her to look at the ground just left of the nose on the next landing, and see if that would help. I said; lets take off again, go around the field, land again, and see what happens. She did what I asked her to do. On the final approach I saw her head turn slightly to the left down, and when the wheels touched the ground they stayed there. Problem solved. She didn`t have another bad landing.

Soon after that Mr. Brewer rode with her a few minutes, came back , landed, taxied up to the other end of the runway, got out, and said; time to solo. She turned out on the runway opened the throttle, and took off, and flew around the field, and landed like a pro. Mr. brewer told her that she did a great job on her solo flight. Go back up, fly where ever you want to go, and enjoy it. She took off, and was gone several minutes, came back, made a good landing, taxied up close to the hanger, and turned to the right, and the plane went into a tail spin. It turned about a round and a half, and stopped. It scared her out of her wits, but it wasn`t her fault. The spring on the left side of the tail wheel broke, and the prop —wash against the right rudder caused the plane to spin to the right. When the plane stopped spinning she got out shaking like a leaf.

She thought she had done something wrong. Mr. Brewer came out of the hanger, and talked to her, and told her that it was not her fault, and said ; lets go up again, and give you time to get over your scare, and you will be alright. They went up, flew around over town, came back. She seemed to be alright. He told her to come back when she was ready, and fly as much as she wanted. Time went by, and she learned that she was pregnant with our second child. She thought flying might harm the baby, and decided not to fly until after the baby was borne. When it came time for our second baby to be borne Lela had a terrible time with false labor pains, and I had to take her to the Baptist Hospital the fourth time before she was borne. We named her Debra Jeanne Graddy. She was a good baby. We had to wait so long for her to be borne. I`m afraid we spoiled her a bit.

With a new baby to take care of Lela didn`t have the time or the inclination to do any flying. I would ask her about it now and then, but she would answer with, maybe next month. It went on like that for a few months. And Lela got a job doing color patching for a Television Manufacturing Plant nearby, and she didn`t have time to fly. Time went by, then she said; I will get back to it later, but she never seemed to find the time, and decided to forget about it for the time being. She got caught up in things that seemed to be more important, and never was able to get back to flying. During the same time period I reached the required number of hours, and passed the required tests to take the Instructors flight test. On the day of the test I went to the instructors office. He took me out to the plane, we got into the plane , took off and flew over to the North Little Rock airport, climbed up to five thousand feet, and the flight test began. He started giving me all kinds of maneuvers to do. I did every maneuver to the best of my ability. Then he said, lets go back to Adams Field.

I flew back to the airport, landed, and we went back to his office. He said; you did well on the test, but I think you can do even better, I would like you to go back, fly six or eight more hours, and come back, and do it again. If you will do that, I think you will make a good instructor. I had been told by other pilots that he never passed anyone on the first try. I went home, and told Lela that I didn`t pass the test. She asked me why I thought I failed the test. I said; well, I`m told that nobody passes the test the first time, with him. I knew if I flew the hours that he asked me to, the G. I. bill would not pay for it. I would have to pay for it myself, and I didn`t have the money. I decided to wait a while, and maybe I could somehow come up with the money, but that didn`t work out. I never did go back. I have often wondered how it would have turned out, had I gone back, and passed the test.

Chapter 24

In the spring of 1954 we bought a lot from Mack Thomas on Henry street, and had a small house moved from Pine Haven, and had it set up on the lot. The movers jacked the house up high enough so I could dig, pour a footing, and build a foundation under the house, and let it down on the foundation. We had been down to visit Papa, and Mama in Senath Mo, where they had been living since they moved there in1949. Papa came home with us to help me dig, and pour the footing. His plan was to help me with the footing, and pour the concrete. When that was finished he would go on down to Atlanta Texas to visit a sister there. One evening after we had finished super, and was sitting around the table, Lela asked him to tell us about his first family. He said; I lost five members of my family in one year. I lost my wife, three children, and my mother to Typhoid fever. He went on to say, I wondered why god would take my loved ones away form me like that. I tried to think of what I must have done to deserve this, but no matter how hard I tried, there was no answer. Then it finally came to me. THE LORD GIVITH, AND THE LORD TAKETH AWAY. When he finished we were all crying. He went on to say. When I married your mother and started having more children I was always afraid if I got close to you, I would lose you just as before. When I got to where I could talk, I said; Papa, I wish I had known this, all through the years, I thought you didn`t love me, and all of my brothers, and sisters thought the same thing. He answered, and said; I wish you wouldn`t tell the others about this. I said Papa, please don`t ask me to keep this a secret, I just can`t do it.

Papa continued to help me until the end of the week. Then I took him to the bus station, and put him on a bus to Atlanta Texas where he would visit with his sister. I started working on my foundation. As I mentioned, before I had watched the brick layers work, and it looked easy to me, but when I started laying brick it wasn`t as easy as it looked. When I would dip some mortar on my trawl, and try to put it on the brick it would slide off of the trawl before I got to the brick. I was getting more mortar on the ground than I was on the brick. I didn`t remember the brick layers having that kind of problems. I tried a lot of different things that didn`t work. Then I tried using common since .If it slides off the trawl, it must not be sticky enough. I mixed up another batch of mortar, and added more mortar mix, and mixed it up. Then when I tried it again the mortar did not slide off the trawl. I had learned the hard way what the brick layer already knew. I went on with my foundation. I was a little slow at first, but I gradually picked up the pace, and soon finished the foundation.

Then I began to lower the house down onto the foundation. With that finished I moved into the house. I could get more work done that way because I could do a little work in the evenings after I got home from work. The next thing I did was build a carport, and storage room on the east end of the house, and put a flat roof on it. after that I moved to the west end of the house, and started the foundation for two large bedrooms, and a good sized bathroom. That project took the better part of a year to build. Dale bought a lot a block to the west of me, and we started swapping work. We would work on his house a while, and then work on mine a while. It was a lot easier that way, because one man cannot build a house by himself. There are certain parts of it that is strictly a two man job.

After I got the house dried in I focused on completing the new bathroom so I could tear out the old bathroom to make room for the kitchen. I finished the bath with ceramic tile, set on a mortar backing, as was all baths in those days. and it is still there looking good today. When we were finished we moved into the house. Then we turned our attention to the outside yard. When we bought the lot, it didn`t have any trees on it. my wife , and I went over to a wooded area below her father, and mother house, in Bryant. We found six trees that we liked. They were three to four inches in diameter. Four of them were red oak, and two were willow oak. We dug them up with a pick, and shovel. We hauled them to our house, three at a time on a two wheel trailer. We dug holes big enough to accommodate the root system, covered them up, and put guy wires on them to keep them from being blown over, and watered them once a week. I also fertilized them each spring with triple thirteen fertilizer. A concrete truck got too close, and killed one tree, and I had one taken down. My neighbor told me one afternoon while I was watering them, that those trees wouldn't be big enough to shade my grave when I died. I`m not dead yet, and the smallest tree is at least [three feet in diameter].

Chapter 25

In 1955 I got involved, along with several others in organizing a Civil Air Patrol squadron at the Benton airport. Dean Carter was named the squadron commander with the rank of Captain. I was named the Flight control Officer with the rank of 2nd Lieutenant. Dale was the Officer in charge of Cadet training, with the rank of 2nd Lieutenant. The duty of the Civil Air Patrol was to fly search, and rescue missions in case of a missing aircraft. Our mission also included taking Cadets up, and giving them some of the principles of flight. We were given a J-5 cub by the Air National guard to use. I was responsible for the plane while we were using it. This took a lot of my time, and money, because we had to pay for the gasoline that it used. It was my responsibility to check out each pilot, and approve his flying ability before he could take up a Cadet. There wasn`t many that wanted to fly the Cadets, and some of them didn`t pass the test. As a result I had to fly most of them myself. After about three years of this I decided I was spending too much time away from home on week ends, so I resigned my job as Flight Control officer.

When I as thirty four ears old I learned that I could go to the Courthouse and take a test to get an equivalency certificate. I had always wanted more education. I went to the Courthouse, and I signed up to take the tests. I started at 8 o clock in the morning. I took test all day, and they told us that we had one more test that we could take the next morning. I went back the next morning, and took the last test. When I got the results of the test, I couldn`t believe it. I had made a B average on the test. Now I had a High School education, and had not gone to High School one day in my life. When I received the certificate I enrolled in some night courses given by the Central Ark University At Benton. just to see if they would honor my certificate of equivalency. They did honor it, and I finished two courses.

In 1958, skiing became a rage, and my family ,and I became addicted to it. It all got me started when my Sister Ruby, her husband Chock, and their children Verva Ann, and Danny came up from Florida to visit Dale, his Wife, and their son Mark Ralph his wife, and their children De-Lane, and Francis. My Wife, and I and our children, Diane, and Debra. For a long weekend. Chock brought his 12 HP Evenrude motor with him. We all went to Lake Watchataw on Saturday. We rented a 14 foot aluminum boat, and proceeded to learn to ski. We let the smaller ones try it first. When they all failed it was time for DeLane to try it. He walked out into the water, put the skis on, got a good grip on the tow rope handle, and said; lets go.! He dragged along through the water until the motor picked up speed, and then he came up out of the water, and skiied out across the lake. Chock pulled him around in a big circle, and brought him back to the bank. Everyone cheered for him, and said; bravo, bravo. He is the best. He took off the skiis, walked up out of the water, and said; uncle Ray it`s your turn!

I went through the same procedure as DeLane, and when I got a grip on the rope handle, I said; hit it, I too dragged through the water until the motor picked up speed, and then I came out of the water, and skiied out across the lake. Chock pulled me around in a big circle, and brought me back to the bank. They all cheered for me, and gave me a big bravo also. When I walked out of the water, DeLane came over, and said ; I knew you could do it. Other members of the family tried it and couldn`t quiet get up, and stay up for any length of time. I`m not sure that getting up, and skiing on the first try was good for me because it started me to thinking that I had to have a boat of my own. Not long after that, Lela`s brother Bob bought a small wooden boat that looked like a racer, that had a twenty five horse power motor, and tried it out, but It didn`t have enough power to suit him. I bought it from him, and repainted it, and used it for a couple of years. It really looked sharp. The first day I took it to the lake, and put it in the water

I realized that the steering cables had been hooked up backwards, and when you tried to turn either way it would turn the opposite direction. I almost ran it into the bank several times before I learned to maneuver it safely. We managed to ski behind it, but it wasn`t easy. Needless to say the first thing I did when I got hone was to redo the steering cables so they turn the boat the way you turned the steering wheel. With that done we had a lot of fun skiing behind it until everyone started to try skiing two at a time. It didn`t have the power to pull two skiers. I traded it in on a 14 ft Styrofoam boat with a 35 H.P. Evenrude motor. We used it that way several years, and then everyone wanted to ski three at a time. I traded that motor for a 65 H.P. Mercury motor with a thirteen degree propeller.

It would pull three skiers out of the water on slalom skies. I kept it as long as I had the boat. We skied for about twelve years all together, most of which was done on lake Hamilton. There were several other people that got into skiing the same time as we did. To name a few, they were Max, and Myerline Wright, Jackie, and Roger, Densil, and Mary Dyer, Denny, and Boe. Boyd, and Bonnie Ward, and Francis. We would go to church Sunday morning with our boats hooked to our trucks or cars, and when services were over, we would go to Farrs Landing on lake Hamilton, ski all afternoon, and drive back to church for the evening service. There was always a bunch of people that came from Little Rock to ski there also. Most of them would bring beer to drink, but we stuck with our cokes, and root beer tea or water. They could not understand how we could have fun without drinking alcoholic beverages, but we told them that alcohol was not a pre-requisite to having fun. I think we may have converted a few of them. We did have a lot of fun, but when our kids grew up, and turned to other interests, we soon found out that it wasn`t as much fun without them with us, and one after the other we quit going to the lake. I sold my boat to my sun in law, and found other things to do.

One day when I got home from a hard days work I told my wife, I have been making a living with my hands, and tools. Starting now, I`m going to begin preparations to make a living with my brain. I had a friend, Ovid Ward who was a Superintendent for his brother Earnest Ward Construction Co. Ovid had been trying to get me to come to work for him, I told him I would work for him one year to get some experience doing commercial construction. I told Fred Parrott I would be leaving after Friday. He wanted to know why I was leaving. I said; I feel that it is time for me to move on. I believe I have the knowledge to supervise a project, and I already have a job with Earnest Ward. I can get some experience doing commercial work, and that is the type of work I would like to do. The following Monday I went to work for Earnest Ward. I told Ovid I wanted him to put me on every different type of work on the project so I could do it all. When my year was up I told him that Friday is my last day to work for you. He said; what do you mean? I said; don`t you remember our agreement? He said; I wish I didn`t, but I do.

I went to work for Herb Davis as project Forman, the following Monday morning. I built two or three houses for him, and then he got a Townhouse project to build on cedar hill road, and he put me on it as Project Superintendent. The project consisted of four two story buildings. With six apartments in each building on two levels with a pool, and a pool house. There was a thirty eight feet difference in floor elevation from the highest to the lowest. It was on a hillside to say the least. We hadn`t been working long on the first foundation when we realized the basement floor level on the plans was at least one foot below the top of a layer of granite. I told Herb what we had run into, and he asked me if I had any ideas on what we could do I told him I had a couple of ideas if the architect would agree to them. We can raise the floor level one foot, or we can spend a bundle of money digging the granite down to the elevation shown on the plans. He said; I will talk to the architect. He came to the project the next morning, and told me he had talked to the architect, and he said; no way, it would cost more to change it than it would to dig out the granite. I said; what do you want me to do. he said; I know a contractor that has a D- 8 dozer I will get him to come down here tomorrow, and look at this.

The next day the contractor met with me, and Herb at the jobsite, and looked at the problem. We had a man on the job with a backhoe. We had him to dig holes in several places to show the guy what we had encountered. He said, that D-8 dozer will rip that granite out of there without opening the governors on the engine. I will bring it down here Saturday, and Sunday. We can rip this out of all four foundations in two days. Herb looked at me, and said; can you be here both days? I said; I sure can. I met him on the jobsite the next day at 8 A.M. He started the dozer, and dropped the ripper down. It bounced along the granite a few yards, and when it got down in the granite it couldn`t move it. He worked all day, and didn`t dig up enough to fill a five yard dump truck. He came back Sunday, and didn`t dig up any more than he did the first day. He said; well I was sure that this dozer would rip that out easy, but it want.

Herb said; I will talk to the architect again, and explain to him what we tried, and it failed. Then it will be up to him to tell us what he wants us to do. After Herb talked to the architect, he told me the architect wanted us to hire a dynamite man that has the credentials to drill, and blast out granite using ammonium nitrate. I looked in the phone book, got a number, and called the man listed in the book. When he answered the phone I told him what my problem was, and he said; yes I can blast out anything. I asked if he had insurance he said; no I don`t. I work by the hour. You will need to furnish the insurance, the ammonium nitrate, the jackhammer. and a man to drill the holes. I told Herb what the man said, ok he said, I will get the fertilizer, rent a jackhammer, furnish a man to drill the holes, and the owner will furnish the insurance. I called the man back, asked him when he could start. He said; I can start tomorrow I Said; be here at 8 A. M.

I called Herb, and told him to get the jackhammer, get the man to run it, The dynamite man will be here tomorrow. When the dynamite man got to the jobsite the next morning he introduced himself as Jim Barlow. I took him down to the basement of the first building, and showed him where I wanted him to start. I introduced him to jack, the man who would drill the holes for him, and told him, to tell jack what he wanted him to do. I told him that I would be somewhere on the project if you need me. Jack started drilling holes, and Jim started laying out areas to drill. It took the better part of the day to get started, but when he got the first area ready he told me he needed about six sheets of plywood to lay over the area as a burden to keep the blast from throwing chunks of granite in the air. I had the plywood hauled down to him, he laid the plywood over the blast area, walked about fifty feet away with the plunger, set it down, yelled, fire in the hole, and pushed the plunger down. The blast pushed the plywood up les than two feet high, and settled back down. There was not one piece of granite thrown in the air.

From then on you could hear the yak yak yak of the jackhammer, the rumble of the plywood being placed over the granite, the sound of Jims Baritone voice, yelling fire in the hole, and the varroome of the blast. This went on for weeks, and months. I had my men move down to the lower side of the jobsite adjacent to Cedar Street, and start working on the footings for a retaining wall that ran the full distance of the two lower level buildings, and was five feet high at one, end, and twenty feet high at the lower corner of the jobsite. When Jim, and my man with the backhoe, and dozer got the basement of the first building blasted, and dozed down to the proper elevation, I moved a crew of men up there to work on the basement foundation. Herb sent Dale to the project to help watch the crew on the first foundation. The additional work required to get down to the elevation shown on the plans put us five to six month behind schedule, and cost the owner a lot of money. He had to pay for a lot of so called damage on houses up above the jobsite. Everyone had some kind of damage. There was no way you could prove that it was already there. The owner paid everybody that had a complaint.

Chapter 26

We finished the project about five months behind schedule. I don`t know how much we were over budget, but Herb told me it came out alright. Herb sent me out to western Little Rock to refurbish a house near Cammack Village. Toward the end of that project I was talking to a man that was sitting next to me in the church choir. He asked if I would like a job with Pickens Bond? Which was the Company he was working for. I answered yes I would. I am about finished with the project I am working on now. The next time I saw Herb I asked him if he had any work coming up for the winter months, he, said no I don`t. I said; I may have a job with Pickens Bond, if I want it. a friend of mine is going to talk to them, and let me know. Before I finished the work for Herb, he told me I had the job, as Forman on a Medical building on Markham street near the War Memorial Stadium He told me to meet the project Manager at the jobsite Monday.

I was there Monday morning at work time. The project Manager wasn`t there, but the Superintendent was. He took me down into the jobsite, and showed me the area that he wanted me to work on. He told me to call the Union hall, and hire a crew of men. Then he took me back to the office and showed me the plans, and turned to the page where the area was shown on the plans, and showed me where the details were. then he said; study the plans, and I will be back after a while. I started looking for the pages he had shown me, and I couldn`t find a thing. I thought to the myself. What are you doing here. Maybe you don`t know enough to be here. About that time a guy came in, and said; are you the new Forman? I said; yes I am, but I may not be here very long. He said; why do you say that? I said; I can`t find the area that he showed me. He laughed, and said; don`t worry about it. I`m the surveyor, and know where it is. I will lay everything out for you when you get started.

He showed me how to find everything that I needed to look at, told me what his name was, and said, if you have a problem I will help you with it. I looked at the plans the rest of the day, studying the details on the columns, and beams that I would be building. The next day the union hall sent me enough men to get started building the forms for the columns. They had been poured up through the floor, and all we had to do was to build forms to extend the column up to the next floor. I continued working on the Medical building for about four months, and they transferred me to North Little rock to help out on the Shorter College apartment project. I worked there about three months, and they sent me to Layfette Louisania as the superintendent of the mall, and small shops at the North Gate Shopping Center. Going to Louisania was like going to a Foreign Country The population there was ninety five % Cagen, and the other five % were on vacation. There was only one man under my supervision that could speak English, and

I chose him for my Forman. They were all very friendly people, but you didn`t need one of them for an enemy. They were also good workers. When I wanted something done I told my Forman what I wanted done, he would then tell them what to do, and how to do it. You never knew if he told them what you told him, but we got along just fine. While I was working there I drove home every week end. The trip was 349 miles one way. I just about wore out a Ford truck going home, and back, while I was there. My brick Forman took me fishing one Saturday We went about twenty miles south, put the boat into a canal, and went another ten miles to the Gulf of Mexico. He took me out in the Gulf to where he had been catching fish. We fished out there two or three hours. We caught a few small fish, but nothing to write home about. Then we went back home. When he let me out where I parked my truck he said; I`m sorry we didn`t catch any fish. I said; don`t mention it. I enjoyed it, and I thank you for taking me. I worked there five months, and then they sent a man to take my place that had more time with the company than I did, and sent me back home.

Chapter 27

When I got home I called, and asked for Bill When he answered the phone I told him who I was, and asked him if he had a project to put me on. He answered, I may have. We are starting a project out toward Lonoke for the Remington Arms Plant He told me to go out I – 40 to mile marker 69, and turn right, and drive out to our office trailers, and ask for Leon. I did as he suggested, and asked for Leon. That's me, he said; what can I do for you ? I said; bill told me to come out here, and talk to you about a job as superintendent. He said; where have you been working? I said; at Layfette Louisana at the North Gate shopping Center. He said; do you have anyone that could vouch for you? I said; yes I do. Your nephew worked for me on the Cedar hill Apartments off Cantrell in Little Rock. I think he would vouch for me. He said; he is working out here for me. He picked up the phone, dialed it, and said; come up to the office. In a couple of minutes he walked in the office, spoke to me. Leon said; would you like to work for this guy? He said; I sure would. He turned to me, and said; you are my field superintendent. When can you start? I said; I just started.

When we moved to Benton we moved our membership from the Bryant missionary Baptist church to the Southern Baptist church in Benton. We attended church there some three years or more. When Lela went to work in Jones grocery store on Edison avenue we got acquainted with Max Wright who was the manager of the store. Max invited us to visit his church, The Sharon Missionary Baptist church on Shenandoah road. We visited Sharon church the following Sunday, and enjoyed it so much that we kept going there, and after almost a year we moved our membership to Sharon Baptist church, and it has been there every sense, except a few times when we would move it to where I was working on a project.

As you drive down I 40 toward Memphis the first thing you see is a tall building reaching up to a height of 205 feet. That is the shot tower where they make ammunition for shot guns, and beyond that are two large buildings. That is only a part of it. The plant is built on 1100 acres of land, has fifty five separate buildings on it, and a railroad spur with a set of a scales built on the end of it that would weigh a box car. The other buildings were scattered out to the south, with the smallest of them all being 10x10 powder storage sheds which were built inside revetments as a means of safety. I would have to say that was the biggest, and best project, I ever supervised. I had over 200 men working directly under me, not to mention all the sub- contractors that I had to deal with, Within the last six months of the completion of the project, the company hired a second superintendent to watch over the outlying buildings on the project. His name was Arnold Sodman. He had retired from another company to the shores of the gulf of Mexico in southern Mississippi, where he moved into a new home. The home was beyond the point of being covered by insurance. He and his wife had only been living in the house a few months when a hurricane hit the coast and completely demolished their home.

One of the company`s officers knew Arnold, from another project they both had worked on, and when he heard of his misfortune he hired Arnold to fill in on the Remington Arms project. When I met him, and talked with him a few minutes, I realizes that he had more going for him than I had first thought. After working with him a while, l learned that he had a way of dealing with people that I had never seen before. He could talk to a sub-contractor about some thing that should be done differently, and convince the guy without a doubt, that his was the better way, and the guy would walk away smiling. I tried to adopt some of the things I learned from him. I was on the Remington Arms Plant Project twenty seven months, when they asked me to build an addition on the Crestwood Apartments behind Hocotts nursery.

When I finished the Apartment addition they had merged with Rector Phillips Morris to build apartments, and adopted the name, Apartment Developers, and set Arnold up as Project Manager for Pickens bond. Arnold asked Bill Echols if he could have me as his Superintendent. Bill said, yes you can, and tell Ray he can come back to Pickens Bond when he gets all the Apartments built I went from there to a condominium development on Rodney Parham Road. I took the project over when the other Superintendent quit. He marked on a progress chart showing what had been done when he left.

After I had been there a week or so, I showed Arnold where he claimed to have been, and where he actually was when l took over the project. Arnold said; you`re right. I knew he didn`t have as much done as he said he did. When I finished the project Arnold took me to an apartment project in Morrilton that needed some repairs. He told me he planned to send Charley watts up there to do the job, and he wanted me to drive up there every once in a while, and check on him. In the meantime he had me watching a Project in Jacksonville. When these were all finished he told me that they were planning on getting out of the business of building apartments. He said; i`m thinking about retiring. I went to Pickens Bond office to talk to Bill Echols, just like he asked me to do, and Bill said; I know I told you to come back here when you finished building apartments, but building has slowed down to a point that we only have one job, and we have every Superintendent on that job except you. I am sorry, but I just don`t have any place to put you."

Chapter 28

I started looking for a job. I signed up for Unemployment Compensation, sent out resumes to every contractor that I could get names of out of the Phone Book, and read the want adds in the newspaper every day for two or three weeks. After I was approved for compensation I began to receive a check each week from that, and that helped put food on the table. Someone gave me the name of Daniel Construction Co that was located in the Summit Building on Univ ersity ave, and Cantrell Road. I went to their Office, and told the secretary I would like to talk to the Personnel Officer. She showed me to his office. I introduced myself, and he said; have a seat. I sat down, and asked if he had any openings for a Superintendent. He said; as a matter of fact I do. he said; do you have a resume? I said; yes I do. I handed him my resume, and waited for him read it. When he finished reading the resume, he said I have two Elementary schools to build. One of them is at Joe T Robinson, and the other is at Gravel Ridge on Hwy. #7 north. He said; you can have either one. I said; Joe T Robinson would be closer for me. He asked me when I could start? I said ; Monday would be good for me.

I started the project the following Monday. The school did not have separate rooms like most schools. There was one big room, and all eight grades were separated into small groups by walkways. I didn`t know that at first. It wasn`t until after the slabs were poured, the tilt slabs were erected, and we were laying out walls for the kitchen area, that I realized that the plans didn`t show any layout for the classrooms. I called the office, and asked my boss if he had a plan showing the classroom wall layout. He said; there are no classroom walls. There is one big room for all the classes. The principal came out to the jobsite to look around one day, and I asked her how it worked without walls between the classrooms. She said ; it works just fine. I said; I don`t see how it could. She said; when we get moved in. I want you to come back to see us, and I will walk you through the large classroom. I think you will be surprised at what you see. I did go back to visit, and she walked me through the classroom, and not one time did I see a student look across the isle to see what was going on in the other classes.

They gave me the responsibility of finishing both schools. One day I would go to Joe T Robinson school in the morning, do whatever was needed there, and go to Gravel Ridge, and take care of any problems they might have there, and reverse the procedure the next day. I continued that schedule until both schools were finished, and turned over to the School Board. Then they sent me to Mountain Home to build a shipping, and receiving building for Baxter Travenoll Loboratories.I spent the first week making preparations to get the building started. They asked if I could get a Forman to work the job, because they needed me to be elsewhere part of the time. I said; yes I can get my brother Ralph. I called Ralph, and asked if he would like to come to Mountain Home, and help me out. He said; yes I will. While I was at home that weekend I called a man, and rented a mobile home that he had there, and moved into it Sunday afternoon. Before the end of the week they told me that they needed me at Cleveland Mississippi on a facility they were building for Baxter Travenoll Laboratories there. We both went home that weekend. Ralph made plans to go back to Mountain home, and I made plans to go to Cleveland Mississippi.

Early Monday morning I headed toward Cleveland Mississippi. The first thing I learned was, it was 200 miles from my house to Cleveland. When I arived at the jobsite I went to the office trailer, and met Bill, the Project Manager. He took me out to the plant, introduced me to the Superintendent in charge of the work in progress, and told him to walk me around over the building, and show me all the work that was going on. That will get you acquainted with where everything is located within the building. He walked me through the building showing me where all the work was being done. There must have been eight or ten different small projects in progress, which was scattered all over the building. While we walked he told me that he would be leaving in a day or two. That told me that he was the man I was replacing. He told me his wife had come to stay through the week, and when she left to go home he would be going with her. I had lunch with them, and met his wife. She was a nice looking young lady. When we got back from lunch I asked him to write down the name of each project, and describe the location of each project.

I spent the afternoon looking for a place to live. About this time Lela bought me a starter set of Northwestern golf clubs so I would have something to occupy my time when I wasn`t working. It took a while for me to get started playing, because I didn`t know where there was a golf Course. I stayed in a motel while I looked for a place to live. When I got to the job the next morning he handed me a list of all the projects in the building, and the location of them. I said; that's what I need. Without this I would never be able to find them. Each evening after work I would look around for a room to rent. After looking for three days I found a room in the Shamrock Apartments. They had suites that you could rent by the month, with kitchen facilities. You had to furnish your own bed clothes. Lela had a job at home, and couldn`t come down with me for a while, but she did come down after a month or two. That made it a lot easier, because I didn`t have to run back, and forth on weekends. Daniel Construction Company`s primary contract was to completely renovate, and enlarge the bottled saline solution fill line including all it`s subsidiaries. on a two story area. All doors, and equipment had to be stainless. All wall finishes had to be epoxy paint without even a pinhole visible. The floors had to be epoxy, trawled to a smooth surface without any holes that germs can hide in.

They shut down the line, and we started breaking out the floor slab, the plumbing, the electrical, and everything that needed to come out all the way to the roof. Bill, and I worked twelve to sixteen hours a day, seven days a week. He worked with the owner Architect, and Engineer, and I worked with the sub- contractors. When we would meet in the corridors he would yell out the answer on something we had a problem on, and I would get the respective contractor to go to work on it. That is the way it worked through the project. Eight weeks after they shut the line down they turned it back on, and started running bottles of saline solution down the line. If we needed to go back into the area to check on something we had to check out a white suit, we called it a rabbit suit, and put it on, along with sanitized boots. Just to go in, and look at something .It would take an hour of our time to go inside to check on an item that would only take a minute to look at. I was there a month or so after that doing miscellaneous projects around over the building. Then they sent me to Henderson Tennessee to help finish a building where they built huge electrical motors. After I was home a week or two I had to go back over there for a week to take care of an item that didn`t work properly.

Chapter 29

When I got back home they called me to go back to Cleveland Mississippi to supervise an addition on the front of the Baxter Travenoll Laboratories existing building. it took me six months to finish that building. Then they sent me around to the back of the building where I started a sewage disposal plant. I had about finished the excavating the sewage pond when a fellow I had worked with before called me, and asked if I would be interested in a job for Construction Advisors who was building a plant for Baxter Travenoll Laboratories at Ash Flat Arkansas? I said; yes I would. He told me that his company was doing the Mechanical work there. The Project Manager for Construction Advisors [Stan Orr]   had asked him if he knew of a good Superintendent that he could hire for that job? He said; yes I know where there is a good one. I will call him, and give him your phone number. He gave me the phone #, and I called him. After we talked a few minutes he asked if I could come up there for an interview. I said; I would like that. I will come home this weekend, and I can come up there Saturday. He gave me instructions on how to get there, and said I will see you in my office Saturday at 2 O- clock. Bring your wife with you. I will make arrangements for a place for you to spend the night.

We got up Saturday morning, did all our chores, and headed for Ash Flat which was about a three, and a half hours drive. We stopped on the way, and ate lunch. We got to his office about one forty five, and he was already there. He invited us in, and we did the introduction thing, He was a fairly short man in his mid fifty`s with graying hair with a small bald spot in the back of his head. He said; come onto my office I started in, and he pointed at Lela, and said ; you too. We went on into his office, and sat down. We talked a short time, and when the interview started he asked Lela as many questions as he did me. He asked all the normal questions that most interviewers do, and I answered each one as truthful as I possibly could, and so did Lala

He leaned back in his chair, looked me in the eye, and said; when can you start? I said; in another week. I will tell my company that I will be leaving at the end of next week. He then said; follow me, and I will show you where you will be spending the night. We followed him until he turned into a driveway. We followed him into the driveway, and stopped. He showed us around through the house, an said; make yourself at home. As he was getting into his car he said; we will pick you up for dinner at 6 o-clock.

We had a great dinner at a nice steak house, and a good nights rest at the house that Stan had secured for us. We got up the next morning, had a good breakfast at a restaurant nearby, and drove back home. When we got home Lela, and I sat down, and went back over the things that had been happening to us in the past three or four days. We both felt good about what we were about to do. We thought it was the right thing to do. I didn`t go back to Cleveland that evening. I got up the next morning, and left home at 4 o-clock in order to get to the jobsite by work time. I didn't tell anyone that I was planning on changing jobs until later in the week. Some of the higher officers in the company came to the jobsite Wednesday, to look things over. After walking over the jobsite we went back to the office, and had a short meeting. They thought everything looked alright, and mention some things that might need improving. I said; you will need to get another Superintendent down here, because I will be leaving at the end of the week. One of them said; why are you leaving? I said; because I have worked three years for the same "salary". I requested an increase in "salary" several times, and was refused. This Company offered me more money. They said; we will pay you through Friday, and you can leave today.

I went to the Motel. packed my belongings, and headed home. The next day Lela, and I drove to Cherokee village to hunt a place to live. We checked with a Real-estate Company, and they gave us a list of houses to look at. We look at three or four houses, decided on one of them, and went back to the Real-estate Co, and paid the rent on it. We told them we would like for the rent to start Jan 1st 1977. They said; that`s fine with us. The house we rented was partially furnished. We spent the night in a Motel, and went home the next morning. On the way home we decided we would rent our home, because the mildew was ruining the sheetrock walls. we finally realized that leaving it empty was worse than having someone living in it. We made a contract with a Real-estate Co to keep it rented for us. We packed all the things we thought we needed in our Ford L. T. D, and the rest of it in our 69 El-Camino on the 31st day of December 1976 and headed for Cherokee Village. We got there in time to move everything out of the vehicles into the house before our good friends Max, and Meyerline Wright Densil, and Mary Dyer got to our house. They drove up from Benton in Max, and Myerline`s new Motorhome to spend the night, and celebrate the new year with us.

We all got in the Motorhome, and went out for dinner over in Hardy. We had a good dinner, and drove back to our new home, and sat around the table talking, drinking coffee, and waiting for the new year. When 12 o-clock came we all yelled, screamed, and hugged each other, and yelled HAPPY NEW YEAR-HAPPT NEW YEAR. Then sat back down, and talked some more. Then it was time to get some sleep. Max, and Myerline slept in an extra bed in the house, and Densil , and Mary slept out in the Motorhome. About 3 o-clock in the morning the door bell rang. I got out of bed, went to the door, and opened it. there stood Densil. He said; I just heard on the radio that a snow storm is headed this way, and said; we had better go home while we can. By that time Max and Myerline was in the living room with us. They all got dressed ,and got into the Motorhome, and headed home, and it was a good thing they did because when we woke up on New Years Day the snow was about 12 inches deep, and still snowing. The snow kept falling until it was 18 inches deep, and this happened January 1st 1977.

We soon got to know our neighbors, and they were all very nice. There was one of them that liked to pick up things for his neighbors if he was going to the shopping center. While the snow was on the ground was a good time to have a good neighbor like him. I don`t know what we would have done without him. The snow stayed on the ground the entire week. I couldn`t get to the job that week. I called Stan every morning and asked him if he thought we could get to the job, and he would say, you couldn`t work if you got there. Then he would say; don`t worry about it, enjoy the snow By Thursday morning I decided I had to try my luck at getting out of the Village. Lela, and I got into the car, and drove down the road a little ways, but when we got to the bottom of the hill, and started up the other side the wheels began to spin, and came to a stand still. We tried to beat the ice off the pavement with a tire tool, but that didn`t work. We very carefully backed down into a driveway, and drove back home, and stayed there.

After a week at home the snow had melted enough for me to get to the jobsite. In all the times that I had changed jobs, this was the first time I had a weeks vacation up front. Monday was my first day on the job. Stan, and I walked over the jobsite to evaluate the damage of the snow, and to estimate the time delay caused by it. We got a man on a loader started to move the snow away from the foundation, and dig trenches to drain the water off of the jobsite. When we got back to the office we looked over the plans, and he explained what had already been done, and where he hoped to go from there. If you have a question please feel free to ask me. He said; I know it will take a few days for you to get your feet on the ground. After that you can run the job in the field, and I will run the office. I said; that sounds like a winner to me. The first few weeks we were there, Stan, and his wife Joann showed us the Village Community Center where you could by groceries, gas up your car, and there was also a very nice Restaurant there also.

Hardy was only a few miles east of the Village where you could find some interesting shops in old buildings that you could brouse through. At the east end of town, and across a creek that empty`s into Spring River was a stake, house owned, and operated by Dusty Rhodes, and his family. They were open only on weekends. Their reputation as being the best steak house in the community was such that they had a full house each Friday, and Saturday. They also furnished the music for their guest each Friday, and Saturday night. The waiting line always extended outside the building. When a table became vacant they would come to the door, and announce we have a table for two, four, six, eight, or whatever the case might be. We were in line one time when the waiting line was moving very slowly. We had been passing the time with people around us when our time was next. The door opened, and the lady announced, I have a table for eight. I held up my hand, turned to the three couples behind us, and said; come on, we`re next. We went in, and sat down, and introduced ourselves.

One of them said; thank you for bringing us in with you. I said; they told us they had a table for eight, and there were eight of us.! We all enjoyed our steaks, and the music as well as talking with our new friends. We saw some of them later in the steak house, and we visited with one couple in their home once when we were driving through Calico Rock where they lived. Spring River runs through hardy, and runs on down toward Walnut Ridge, and empties into Black River near Black Rock. The north end of Spring River starts at Mammoth Springs where the water spouts up out of the ground form where, nobody knows, and forms a lake. The lake runs over the dam, and becomes the Spring River. The water in the river never gets any warmer than 58 degrees in the summer. Its' almost too cold to swim in, but the trout fishing is usually good. Stan, Joann, Lela, and myself went up on the River one Saturday where the water was running over the shoals, and fished for trout, and waded around in the cold water. We didn't catch many fish, but we had fun,

Stan was born, and raised in New York City, and had put up buildings there. His Company had contracted to build a plant for Baxter Travenoll Laboratories at Ash Flat, and transferred him to their subsidiary Construction Advisers, and sent him to Ash Flat to do the job. He told me that he wondered what he had done to be sent to a hick town in Arkansas to do a job. After he had been here a little while he began to like the place. He told me he had learned one thing about the people in Arkansas. If they told you that they would do some thing they would do it, and if they said; I will not do that, they will not. He bought some fishing tackle, and started fishing. He had to go to Hardy to the Post Office to get his mail for the office. He would take his tackle and fish a little in Spring River each time he went to the Post Office. Sometimes I think he went to the Post Office when he didn't really did need to go. He once told me that they would not ever get him to come back to New York to work again. There were two Golf Courses in the Village, and I got a discount, because I lived there. and I played any time I got a chance.

Doyle, and Billie Wilson came up to spend the weekend with us once while, we were there, and Doyle, and I played a round of golf on Saturday. Neither of us scored very well, but as they say, a bad day on the golf course is better than s good day on the job. We also took them to the steak house at Hardy Saturday night, where we all enjoyed the steak, and the music, played by the Dusty Rhodes family. It was fun having them for the weekend.It was a pleasure to work with Stan at the project. He did exactly what he said he would do. He ran the office and let me run the work in the field. We had a progress meeting each Tuesday with the sub contractors, and discussed if each contractors work was on schedule. If anyone was behind schedule, they were told to do whatever it took to bring their work back on schedule. And we held them responsible. The Project was approximately 80 % complete when two officers from the higher echelon in the Company came to the jobsite, and requested a meeting with all of the supervisors on the project

We called all the superintendents into the office, and had them to sit down at the table. Stan turned to one of the officers, and said; you have the floor. The officer said; Gentlemen we want you to shut the job down. Everybody`s mouth flew open, he said; we the upper echelon of the Company don`t know what we want to use this building for. The lower echelon of the Company has planned, and contracted with you to build this project without our knowledge. We asked each contractor to give us an estimated schedule of what they needed to safely shut down their portion the of work. Some types of work could be shut down immediately, and some had to wait on others before they could bring their work to a halt. The electrical contractor had some loose ends to complete before he could bring it to an end. The Mechanical contractor had all of his H. V.A. C. units set on the roof, and each unit was at a different level of completion. We also had to make a maintenance contract with the mechanical contractor to periodically inspect the units, and lubricate all parts necessary to prevent rust. When we received this information Stan, and I worked out a schedule, and time of [forty five days] to safely shut the project down.

The contractors all worked together to bring all the different types of work to an end, and avoid any one having to wait on the other. One by one each contractor finished his part of the work, and left the jobsite. It was my job to inspect, and approve each contractors work, and make a note of the completion date on the schedule. When the last contractor completed his work, with my approval left the jobsite. Stan, and I walked over the jobsite to make sure that all useable material was properly stored. When we got back to the office, Stan said; well Ray I guess that's all for you here. Why don`t you go load up your things, and move back home. Baxter Travenoll has awarded Construction Advisors the remaining jobs at their Cleveland Mississippi Plant. I want you to go down there as soon as you can to finish the work that we have there. I will stay here and close the office, as soon as I can get the people from the home office to come down here for a walk through the project, and give them a copy of the completion dates on the schedule, so they can pay us, and I can pay the contactors. Call me when you get home, and get your phone reconnected.

Chapter 30

I had previously called my renters and told them that I would need the house, and gave them a two weeks notice. I called the utility office in Benton, and asked them to turn the utilities back on, and put them back in my name When we got home, and got everything unloaded. And put in it`s proper place, I called Stan, and told him that I was all set to go to Cleveland. He said; go on down there Monday. When you get there go to the same office that you had when you left to come up here, and work with our Superintendent the remainder of the week, and I will come down the following Monday. I did as Stan asked me to do, and the Superintendent told me Thursday afternoon that he was going for a job interview the next day, and if it went well, he would not be back Monday. I assumed that he got the job because he didn`t show Monday morning. When Stan got there Monday I told him what had happened, and he said; I had planed on giving you the job anyway. We walked through the building, and discussed what needed to be done. Before he left he told me that he was going to Marion North Carolina to do some work in one of Baxter Traveoll Laboratories Plants there, and he would keep in touch.

I continued working at the Plant at Cleveland Mississippi finishing the various jobs that we were doing throughout the building, and going back out to the sewage Disposal control building to clear up some miscellaneous items that were missed on the punch list. When I first went back to Cleveland I was staying in a Motel, and the Company was picking up the tab, but after a while they told me that I would need to find other accommodations, and they would pay me perdiem. I found a housekeeping unit in the same motel that I lived in when I was there before, and Lela came down a few days later. A few days after New Years 1978, Stan called, and told me to go to the Memphis Office of Morse Diesel, and talk to them about doing the punch list on a six story building they had lust finished for the Commercial Appeal

Newspaper. I went to the Office of Morse Diesel, and talked to them, and they said; yes we want you to work out the punch list. I called Lela, and told her that I would be staying the rest of the week in Memphis, and I would see her Friday evening.

Lela stayed there in Cleveland until I finished the punch list except a couple of times when she went home for a few days. I met with all the Contractors that had worked there, and told them that I wanted them come back, and work off every item that they had on the list. About half of them said; we have already worked ours off. Like an idiot I believed them, and worked with the others. When we got all of the items marked off I called the Architect , and asked him to come, and take a look at the building. He came the next day, and said; lets start at the top. We rode the elevator to the sixth floor, and started checking off the items that had been done. When we got about three quarters through the sixth floor he turned to me and said; this is not complete, get the contractors back, and go over it again. I apologized to him for getting him out there too early, and assured him that when I called him again it would be completely ready.

I called a meeting with every contractor that had a contract to do work on the project, and invited them to be at the jobsite at 8:00 A,M. the next day. They all showed up on time the next morning. I said; good morning gentlemen. The first day I was here I asked all of you to work out every item on the punch list. Some of you said; you already had. Well I realized yesterday that you had lied to me when the architect told me the building was not ready for him to inspect. Starting right now we are going to go back through the building one floor at a time. My company has held a portion of your money until all punch list items are complete, and approved by the architect. I will be there with you every day checking each item off the list. I have my thumb on your money, I can assure you that you will not see a penny of it until the punch list is completed, and approved by the architect. They all agreed, and started working on the punch list on the first floor. As each contractor finished each floor I would walk through with their supervisor, and check each item with him.

When we reached the sixth floor, and I had checked off each supervisors items. I called the architect, and asked him to come, and look. He came the next day, and as before we started on the sixth floor.

We had hot covered more than half the floor when he turned to me, and said; it looks good. There is no reason to look any further. Overall it took six weeks to work off the punch list. I enjoyed being there, and most of all I met a lot of nice people there. One of their supervisors took me through the plant, and showed me the different phases that is required to turn out a Newspaper. While I was there I was fortunate to see a building being imploded not more than thirty feet from the one I was working in. They gave us a warning about when it would happen, and we stood outside where we could see better. When the man pushed the plunger the building began to quiver, and fall inside of itself. It was over in a matter of seconds, and what was once a building was reduced to a pile of rubble.

I drove over to Morse Deisel, and told them the building was finished, and approved by the architect. They thanked me for doing the job, I said; I was glad to do it. I called Lela, and told her I was finished in Memphis, and asked her what she thought about going home that day. She said; you know that there is snow on the roads. I said; yes I know, but I thought it might be worn off by the traffic by now. Why don`t we try it, and if it gets too bad we will get a Motel room, and spend the night. Can you throw our belongings in the car, and meet me at the junction of sixty one, and forty nine highways, and we will go on home together. She said; yes I guess I can. When we both got to the rendezvous point we got out of our car, and hugged, and did a little mouth to mouth resuscitation, and got back in our car, and started toward home. We both had C-B. radio`s in our cars, and we could communicate with each other. Lela was ahead of me because I wanted her where I could see her. Everything was alright until we got to Binkley. I called her, and suggested that we get on Highway 70, and see how much snow there was on it. when we got to Hazen we stopped, and got something to eat. While were there we heard some one say that it wasn`t too bad on the freeway. We decided to try it. I might add it was dark when we got out on I 40. It wasn`t bad slick, but the snow had frozen after being rutted out by the traffic during the day, and it was like driving over a pile of rocks. I got ahead of Lela so I could run interference for her. We slowed down to about thirty miles per hour, and kept moving as best we could toward Little Rock. When we got closer to the Little Rock the traffic got heavier. As I drove by the junction of 67, 167 I could see cars sliding every direction, then I heard Lela say OOO0000 a car is sliding strait at me, then silence,------finally I heard her say its` alright he missed me, and I said; thank god. We made it through Little Rock on I 30 to Benton, and breathed a sigh of relief when we drove down the off ramp to Jefferson street across Jackman street to Henry street, and home.

We didn`t take anything out of the cars, and went into the house. We both said; thank you lord, for keeping us safe .we want do that again. Then we fell into bed, and passed out. As soon as I got the phone hooked up I called Stan at Marion North Carolina, and told him we were back home in Benton ar. He asked me about the job in Memphis. I told him that it was finished, and approved by the architect and the guys at Morse Deisel was happy with it. He asked me how I felt about going to Hampden Sidney Virgina to build a field house facility for an all boys college. I said; that sounds good to me, but I need to talk to Lela about it. I gave him my phone number and he said; I will call you when I know more. I said; I will be waiting for your call.

Chapter 31

The next time he called he told me that we had the job at Hamden Sydney College and wanted me to do the job. He suggested that Lela, and I would drive to Marion North Carolina. As soon as we could make arrangements with a Real-estate Company to handle the rental of our houses we loaded up the car, and headed toward Marion North Carolina. When we got to Marion we secured a room in the Apricot motel, and called Stan to let him know that were there. He invited us over to their house for dinner. While we were there we made some plans for going to Virginia. We stayed there a couple of weeks while I helped Stan at the plant. Then Lela, and I went on up to Farmville Virginia, and secured a room in the Wyanoke Hotel. The hotel was a building that was probably built in the early 1800. It had an elevator that was operated by a person. When you walked inside, it was like walking back into the past. The rooms were very nice, and the staff was as nice as the rooms.

There was a restaurant on the first floor where you could get about anything you wanted to eat. We had our sheltie puppy Ginger with us that we had brought from Arkansas, and the staff treated her like she was human being. The next day we started looking for a place to live. The first place we went was a Real-estate office. The Realtor started telling to us about what he had available. He said; we have a hauce on this street, and a hauce on that street. It finally dawned on me that he was telling us where he had a house. He didn`t have anything that we wanted, but he did tell as about a place that night have something we would like. We went from one place to another until we found a house we liked. It had some nice big rooms on the first floor, and had a partial attic with an extra bed room. we told the man that we would take the house, and paid him the first months rent. 1 called Stan, and gave him the phone number at the Wyanoke Hotel, and told him that we had rented a house. He told me he would drive up to Farmville on Monday, and we would do some preliminary planning to get the project started.

He arrived in Farmville late in the day Monday, secured a room in the hotel, and called us to let us know that he was there, and said; I will see you in the morning at breakfast. We met him in the restaurant the next morning, had a good breakfast, and discussed the plan for the day. The first stop was the City Hall where we secured a Permit for the Project. We were told that the County would do the inspections on the Project. We went to the Court House, and met with the inspector, and discussed how we would like to schedule the inspections. He said; when you get ready for an inspection. Call me, and I will be there in a matter of hours. I said; that sounds good to me. Then we drove over to the College and met with the Financial Officer, and discussed how his department would fit into the scheme of things, and the sequence, and method of payment. He introduced us to his Secretary, and took us over, and introduced as to the President of the Callege. Stan explained the fast tract method of building to him.

For instance Construction Advisors would make a contract with an owner to build a project for that owner, then they would send out invitations to prospective bidders on the dirt work, the foundation, the concrete, and structural steel before the architectural plans were started. This method made the project move faster because these contractors could be well on their way to completion before the architectural drawings were finished. That was the kind of contract we had with the College. Then we went to the proposed site, and looked it over. As we walked back up the hill, Stan said; by the time you get back we I will have an office trailer moved in for you right over there. We went back to the hotel, and spent the night, got up the next morning had breakfast, and headed toward Marion North Carolina. Stan had told me the night before that we would drive back to his house, and leave my car there. He would take us to Ashville, and put us on a plane to Little Rock.

There will be a rental car waiting for you there. When you get home call this moving Company, and have them to send someone to pack your things, and load them on their van, and bring them to your house in Farmville Virginia. When we got back home we called the moving Company, and got them started packing our things. While they were doing that we visited everyone we could because it would be a while before we would be back. I left my Elcamino with James, and Debbie, and told them to use it any time they needed it. When the movers got the van loaded, and pulled away from our house we said ;good bye to James, Debbie, and the girls, and James took us to the Airport. We went in, and boarded the plane for Ashville North Carolina. Stan was there waiting for us when we got off the plane. He took us home with him, and we stayed the night with Them. Joanne treated us to a dinner, fit for a King, and queen. Early the next morning we put ginger in the car, and we were off to Farmville Virginia.

When we got to Farmville we got a room at the Wyanoke Hotel where we would wait for them to call when they were there, and ready for us to go over, and open the house so they could unload the Van. The movers put all the furniture pretty well in place, but the other things were sitting all around the floors in every room in the house. We spent the rest of the day putting things away the best we could, and out of the way. Then we went shopping for groceries. We brought some of the things with us, but we had to get almost everything else to cook with. I got up the next day, and went to the jobsite. The office trailer was there as Stan said it would be, with the power, and phones hooked up. The excavation contractor was already there working on the building pad. When we entered the Office trailer we found a set of plans lying on the table The building site was down behind a bank. The bank had to be cut down to make the building pad. The bank was sloped down toward the building with a set of steps leading down to the level of the first floor. People diving into the College Campus would only see the roof of the building, and there was a reason for that. All the existing buildings on the campus was built in the 1800 hundreds, and had walls of brick, twelve inches thick, three story`s tall with a tile roof. The hitching post, and rails were still there if you wanted to tie your horse to them.

Chapter 32

I introduced myself to the supervisor of the excavation work, and told him I would be there full time if he needed any assistance with anything. The job got off to a slow start, but there was a lot of drainage, and sewer lines that had to be installed before the foundation could be started. Once that was done the progress began to move along at a faster pace. Stan had set up a new office in Rock Hill South Carolina, and he would drive up once every week or two, and walk over the project with me. The second time he came up he brought me a 1978 model Fremont ford Station Wagon for me to drive while I was there. He said; you use this any way you want. If you, and Lela want to go on a weekend trip, you drive this Station wagon, and when you fill the gas tank, charge it to the company. When he got ready go back to South Carolina, we took him to the Airport at Lynchburg Virginia to catch a plane to Charlotte.

The building was 700 feet long, 128 feet wide, with three basketball courts that would convert to tennis courts, five raquetballand courts and a Junior Olympic swimming pool, with an office area located midway on the second floor. Hamden Sydney was the pride and joy of the people who lived within a fifty-mile radius. They would tell you about all the governors, representatives, senators, presidents, and any other Famous person who came out of that College. They treated us like we were the King, and Queen, because I had been sent there to build a new Field House for their College As soon as we got settled in our new surroundings we began looking for a golf course to play golf on. Some one told us about the Longwood Golf course, and told us how get there. The first time that we had time we loaded our clubs in the car, and drove over to the Longwood Golf course, and went into the clubhouse. We met the club Pro, and told him that we had just moved to Farmville to build a new Field house facility for Hamden Sydney College.

He showed us around the place, and said; put your clubs on a cart, and play a round on me. We put our clubs on the nearest golf cart, and drove over to the first tee box, and pulled out our drivers, and started playing golf. We had a nice round of golf, and enjoyed it very much. we went inside, and thanked the Pro. for treating us so nice. He said; don`t mention it. I said ; I noticed several dogs out on the course. He said; yes, most of them or mine. I asked him if we could bring our Sheltie with us, and let her ride with us in the cart. He said; sure bring her with you. From then on we brought her with us as long as we played the course.

They treated us like Royalty, Not long after we were there the Football coach came by to give me season tickets for all the games that season, and the Finance Officer invited me to join the Country Club out north of Farmville. I thanked him for the invitation, but I said; I will think about it. After that he would ask me about it every time he saw me. Finally I said; I don`t think I have the money to do that.! He said; if I told you that I would fix it so you could, would you do it? I said; yes I would. Two hours later Stan called, and said; do you know what kind of people you are dealing with up there, I said; what do you mean? He told me that john called him, and told him to raise your Salary enough for you to join the Country club, and pay your membership dues as long you are there. I said; are kidding me? He said; no I am not kidding. I called John, and said; do you really mean what you told Stan? He said; I certainly did. Why don`t you, and your wife come out to the Club Sunday afternoon, and I will show you around. Sunday afternoon found as on our way to the golf course. When we walked into the Club House, John saw us coming, and met us half way across the room. He said; come with me. I will show you the course. He took us around to the back of the building, and put us in a golf cart for four people, and drove us all over the golf course. Then he asked if we had our clubs with us. I said ; yes we do. We got our clubs of the car, and put them in a cart. He said; the first four holes are full, let`s go around to number 6 and start there. He said; go down to #6 hole, and hit away, and I will see you when you get back to Club house. We did as he had told us, and when we got to the tee box it was no more than 20 feet from a lake.

I teed up the ball, and swung as hard as I could, and the ball went into the water three times before I got one over the lake. I turned around toward Lela, and said; you`re up. She said; not on this side.! We drove around to the other side of the lake, and found my ball, and both hit from there. We continued playing one hole after the other until we got to # nine green, near the Clubhouse. When we finished putting, we drove to the parking lot, put out clubs in the car, drove back around, and parked the cart, and went inside. John met us there, and asked how did you do? I said; not so good. Number 6 hole beat me good. He said; we`ve all been there done that,! He said; lets go over there, and get you signed up. We went with him over to a desk, and went through the Membership sign up procedure, signed the document, and paid the fees. John shook both our hands, and said; welcome to the club.

Chapter 33

Virginia is a Historical state. Everywhere you go you see something that happened during the Civil War. We lived near one of the most famous sites in the state. Appomattox was only 30 miles from where we lived. We went there several times while we lived in the state. The first time we went to Appomattox we were amazed at what we saw. It was like walking back in time. All the buildings were the shape, and style of the Nineteenth Century. We went to the ticket booth, and bought our tickets, and went into a theatre to watch a movie. The movie showed General Robert E Lee surrendering to General Ulyses S Grant. General Lee offered his sword as was the custom, and General Grant said; put it back in your scabbard. We will sit down as equals, and talk about a treaty. Your soldiers have fought gallantly, and they have earned their freedom I suggest that tomorrow morning you tell your soldiers to march up the hill with their the riffles at rest, and 1 will tell my soldiers to form a line on each side of the road with their riffles at rest. Then you may have your soldiers to march up between the lines, stack their riffles, and walk away as free men.

I was very much moved by the gallantry of General Grant. Then we went to the house where all these things took place. There were the two Generals setting looking at each other across a table. Lying on the table was a copy of the treaty that each had signed over 100 years ago. We also went to a building where all the Civil War memorabilia was displayed. They had everything from a home made tooth pick to a full length soldiers armament. The area was laid out to look like an army camp. The officers had their houses in one area, the soldiers had their living quarters in another area, the livestock had barns to stay in, and the dogs had their dog houses. They had everything there that any other small village would need to live a good life. They also had a Chapel where they could go to worship. Almost every time we went by we would drive through, and look around. We couldn`t help thinking about how life must have been back in those days, when the only way there was to travel was to ride a horse a wagon or walk. None of the above appeals to me. I think I will stay here in the Twenty First century even if everything here is in the biggest mess we have had in decades.

Another interesting place to visit in Virginia is Monticello, which was built by Thomas Jefferson. He began building in 1770 on land he inherited from his farther. The Mansion which he designed in detail took years to complete. But part of it was ready for occupancy when he married Martha Wayles Skelton on June 1 1772. They had six children of which only two lived to adulthood. His wife died in 1782. Jefferson was the third President of the United Sates, and served two terms, from 1801to1809. We went to see Monticello twice while we were in Virginia. The first time we went by ourselves. We went on the tour through the Mansion, and viewed his accomplishments, especially all of his inventions, and his improvements on several things that others had patented. It was hard to believe that one man could do so many things in one lifetime. The second time we went we had our two daughters Diane, and Debbie with us. They had flown up to Virginia to spend a few days with us, and we told them they must see Monticello. they enjoyed the Mansion as much or more than we had, and they kept finding things that we had not seen the first time.

The one thing that we enjoyed more than anything else was the twenty eight day clock. The face of the clock could be seen on the east side of the Mansion. It was 8 ft, in dia, located on the outside of the gable with weights hanging from cables that went down to the basement floor. The clock showed the month, the week, the day, and the hour, and would chime on the hour, half, and quarter hour. It was an ingenious piece of machinery.

Before we went to Virginia Stan called, and asked me how much vacation time I had. I told him I had almost three weeks. He said; why don`t you take a week of it now, and when you get to Virginia, and get the field house moving along smoothly I will get someone to come up there, and watch it while you, and Lela take about a ten day vacation. After that I will make sure you get an opportunity to use all of your vacation time. We had been in Virginia about a month, and a half when I told him I was ready to take the ten day vacation we had talked about He asked me when I wanted go. I told him that we would like to go the second Monday in June he said; that sounds good. We got a travel agency to make us an itinerary so we would know where we should be each day, but we didn`t stay with it all the time. As soon as my relief got there Monday I walked through the building with him pointing out the problem areas to pay special attention to, and gave him a list of contractors telephone numbers if he needed one.

With that done I got in my car, and drove off the jobsite. We went by the dog kennel, and left ginger with them. We had found a good place to leave her. They had two girls that took a liking to ginger, and they would keep her in their home when we left her with them. We headed north through Virginia with hopes of getting to Falls Church Virginia the first day. We arived there late in the evening, got a motel room, something to eat, and went to bed early. We wanted to get up early the next morning to go into Washington to see the sights. The next morning we were up early, ate breakfast, and caught a train to down town Washington. D.C. we didn`t know what to look at first, we walked up, and down the mall, went up in the Washington monument, and went to Lincoln Memorial Then we walked up to the Capitol, and looked around up there. It was closed to the public, and we couldn`t go inside. After that we wondered from one place to another looking at whatever looked interesting.

After lunch we spotted a sign reading the National Museum of Art. we went inside, and I have never seen such an array of art in my life. There was a huge opening down the center of the building, and at the far end you could see a painting of a beautiful woman that almost reached the ceiling. You could look at the paintings in one huge room, and walk back to the center of the room, and there was that beautiful woman again. It took us all afternoon to go through the building, and when we got to the end of the building there was that woman painted on the end wall of the building. We decided we had enough for one day, went back to the mall, and caught the train back to our motel. Before went to bed that night, we decided to stay in Washington another day. There was a lot of things to see that we didn`t have time for the first day, We had a good nights sleep, and caught the train to the mall in Washington D.C. We went strait to the Smithsonian Institution`s Museums` including the National Museum of Natural History, the National air, and space Museum. The National Museum of the American Indian, and the Smithsonian Institution building. They were all very interesting, but the one that interested me the most was the National Air, and Space museum. There was all kinds of old Vintage Airplanes. Being a pilot I was interested in every one of them.

The farther we went into the building the more modern they were, and I had to look at every one of them. We eventually came to the space age area, where they had models of everything used in space I was in space Haven. We were allowed to walk through the space vehicle, see where the crew ate slept, and did their daily individual chores that contributed to the overall operation of the spacecraft. It was almost noon when we came out of the Smithsonian building. We found a huge Restaurant where the Senators, Representatives, and their workers came to eat lunch. We had to wait in line a bit, but we got seated at a table in a reasonable amount of time, and had a good lunch. After that we went out on the mall, and I ran around a section of the mall, just to be able to say, I ran on the mall in Washington D.C. then went to the Museum of Natural History, and spent a some time there. Then we rode a small shuttle to the Arlington National Cemetery, and rode around through it looking at the different things of interest. Then we rode the shuttle back to the mall, and caught the train back to the motel.

We spent another night in the same Motel, got up the next morning, and drove over into Pennsylvania, and got on I – 81. We drove on past Harrisburg, and spent the night in a small town in Pennsylvania. There was a gasoline shortage at the time, and we had to make sure we stopped where there were plenty gas stations so we could get fuel for the next day. We got lucky we found a station with gas, and filled up the tank. We were up early the next morning ready to get started on another day of driving, and looking at country that we had not seen before. We were driving down I- 81 enjoying the countryside when we saw a sigh that read state highway #69 exit one mile. Lela said; I wonder where that road goes.! I said ; we will see. I took the exit off, and we found ourselves driving down a tree lined highway. After diving a few miles we came to a T intersection. On our right was a restaurant. Since we didn`t know where we were we decided to eat lunch there. While we were eating we noticed someone outside hitting golf balls.

When we got ready to leave I stopped at the counter to pay the bill. When I walked outside Lela was talking to man on the sidewalk. She motioned for me to come over there. I walked over to them, and she said; do you want to play golf? I said; I sure do. this man can show us a good golf course. We got in the car, and followed him a little ways on a paved road until he stopped. He pointed at the top of a hill, and said; that is the White Burch golf course on top of that hill. Take the road to the left, and it will take you to it. We thanked him for the information, and drove up to the clubhouse. We got out of the car, went in, asked about playing golf. The man behind the counter asked if we wanted to play nine or eighteen holes? I said; nine holes will be fine. We paid the green fee, went out to the car, got our clubs out of the trunk, put them on a cart, and started paying golf. We enjoyed playing nine holes of golf, and drove 360 miles that day. Lela, and I talk about playing golf there every now, and then.

After we left the golf coarse we drove until we came to a nice looking little town in New York where we spent the night. We gassed up the car before we selected a motel for the night. We were up early the next morning as usual, ready to hit the road. We drove across the corner of New York. Bypassing New York City By about 100 miles. We had already been there, and done that several years ago. We had flown to New Jersey to visit our daughter, and her husband that was stationed in a camp in New Jersey, they had taken us to New York. We had gone as far as we could drive into the city, parked the car, and rode a bus to Radio City Music Hall, where we saw the Rocketts, a stage show, and a movie. When we came back outside the sidewalk was full of people. Lela wanted to window shop, but a Police Officer told her that she had to ,move on. at the same time was trying to get her to go over one block, so I could show her Times Square. She got so shook up about both of us talking to her at the same time. She said; lets get out of here. I wouldn`t live here if I had to crawl through the Lincoln Tunnel.

Now lets get back to where we were before I started chasing a rabbit. We drove on through New York into Connecticut, and kept going until late in the evening, we secured a motel room, and spent the night there. We were on the road early the next day driving through Rhode Island in an effort to get to the eastern seaboard, and drive along close to the Atlantic Ocean in hopes of finding a fishing village that we could stop, and visit with some of the people there, and see how people lived on the east coast. We did find a nice little village with a Motel that had a vacancy. we got a room there. After we had something to eat we walked around the village, talking to people. They were friendly enough, but I think they thought we talked finny, but that was alright we thought they talked funny also. We left the next morning thinking those people are a little different from us, but they are O. K.

We traveled up through Massachusetts into New Hampshire where we spent the night. The Motel we stayed in was just inside the border line between New Hampshire, and Maine. According to Our itinerary we would go to Portland Maine, but we decided to only go a few miles up the coast, turn into the beach which was covered with small stones. We were a little disappointed because we expected sand. We had not seen a rocky beach before. We turned around, and went back through Portsmouth, and headed west across New Hampshire into Vermont where we began to see wooded areas with fast flowing streams coming out of the valleys from the north. We also began to see covered bridges across some of the creeks, cricks, or branches, whatever is the proper name. Lela just had to stop at one of them, and wade out into the cold swift water, and of course I had to do the same. We also had to stop at the first covered bridge, walk out on it, look at how it was built, and drive across it because we had never drove across one before. We really enjoyed driving across Vermont.

Soon we were in upper New York driving west on I-90 headed for Nigeria Falls. We arived there late in the afternoon, and checked in. The person at the counter gave us the key to the room, and told us where to park our car. We followed the instructions, got our luggage out of the car, rode the elevator up to the proper floor, found our room number unlocked the door, and entered the room. As soon as we got our things put away we went over to the window, and looked out at the falls. The first thing I noticed was the water was running north. I said; the water is running up hill.! Lela said; it can`t be,! But it is I said! She said; you`re turned around. I don`t think so, but I`ll find out tomorrow. We got cleaned up, went down to the restaurant, and had dinner. It was a very nice place to eat, and we enjoyed the meal. When we finished eating we went back to our room, watched T. V. for a while, and went to bed. We got up the next morning, went down stairs, ate breakfast, and caught a tour bus that would take us over the river to the Canadian side

The first stop we made I asked the tour guide why the river was running up hill? She said; you are on top of the world. All of the water that comes over the falls goes down hill into the St Laurence River, and runs down, and empties into the Atlantic Ocean. I don`t know about you, but I didn`t know that. It`s only 9 O- clock, and I have learned something new. The tour bus took us to all of the places of interest, and there were a lot of them. We were running a little late getting there, because we had celebrated our thirty second Wedding Anniversary in May. Better late than never they say, and we were having a wonderful time, even if it was late.

The next day we took another tour bus on the American side which included getting on a boat that took us around to several places along the river, up close to the falls, and stopped. The tour guide brought out slicker suits, and told us to put them on. Then she said; are you ready for this? We`re going under the falls. The Captain slowly moved the boast up close, opened the throttle, slammed into the wall of water, and seconds later we were behind the falls. The captain maneuvered the boat around behind the falls, and with a shout from the tour guide, [get ready] the boat slammed back though the wall of water to the outside world again. This was the biggest thrill of all. This was also the last stop of the day. The bus took us back to the Motel, as we all filed out we each thanked the driver, and tour guide for a wonderful day. We went up to our room, rested for a while, went down to the Restaurant, ate an early dimmer, and walked out to look at the falls one last time just before sunset. As we slowly walked back to our room we agreed that this was the best two days of our vacation.

We spent one more night in Niagara Falls, and headed south across New York toward Virginia. We found the state to be very interesting. After a few hours of travel, we began to see grape vineyards on each side of the road. When we stopped for gas we asked the service station Manager about the vineyards, and he told us that New York was one of the largest grape growers, and wine producers in the United States. That's another thing I didn`t know. We continued driving south trough the state into Pennsylvania, and after a while we got on the Pennsylvania Turnpike, and stayed on it the rest of the day. Lela always kept the atlas by her side to keep us going the right direction. In the late afternoon she got it out to find us a place to stay the night. After looking at it a few minutes she said; I can`t believe this.! I said; you can`t what? ! There is a small town up ahead that has 32 Motels. I said; what is the name of it? she said; the name is Bedford. I said; we should stop there.! We shouldn`t have any trouble finding a Motel.

We got off of the turnpike at Bedford, found a room in the first Motel we stopped at. We asked the proprietor where we could find a place to get a good steak. She said; right across the street.! The place she pointed to was a concrete block building with no paint that would pass for anything other than a steak house. When we got settled into our room we decided to go across the street, and see what the place looked like. When we reached the entrance, opened the door, and stepped inside we couldn`t believe our eyes. Everything in the place was high class. It looked like a Restaurant you might see in the movies. The carpet felt like it was two inches thick. A waitress directed us to a table, handed us a menu, and said; I`ll be back to take your order in a few minutes. When she came back to take our order we both ordered a Sirloin steak. She asked how we would like it cooked ? I said; make mine medium, and Lela said; make mine medium well. She brought our steaks in a short time, and when we took the first bite we knew we had come to the right. When we finished eating we told the girl, this is the best we`ve had in years.

When we went back to the motel we asked the clerk why there were so many Motels in town ? she said; this is a ski Resort. There are some good Golf Courses here also. We decided to play a round of golf the next day. We got up early, ate breakfast, and drove to the nearest golf course. We walked around looking at what we could see of the course. Then we went into the clubhouse, paid our green fees, and started playing golf. It was a nice course, well laid out, and not a lot of water hazards. There wasn`t many players on the course. We were able to take our time, and enjoy being out there. When we finished playing golf we drove around town to see the sights. We came upon a huge white building that caught our attention. It was located off the road a good distance, and it looked like it might be a building of some importance. We asked one of the local people about it, and was told that it was the Bedford Springs Hotel, and it had been built in the eighteen hundreds. The water from the springs was found to have a healthy effect on those who bathed in it. The word spread about it`s healthful effects, and

121

people came to the springs from as far away as Pittsburg, New York, and Washington D. C. to bathe in the springs. Several years later it was refurbished by a new owner, and renamed Bedford Springs Resort.

We were also told about the Old Bedford Village which was built by bringing old buildings from the County into the city, placing them on new foundations, and thereby forming a Village, that was a mirror image of any village that was built in the eighteenth Century. We decided to stay another day to see the Village. You could enter the village by crossing a covered bridge, go on by a covered wagon, on up to the gift shop. Of course Lela had to go in, and look around. There were so many things to look at we didn't know what to look at first. I believe Lela picked up half of everything in there, and looked at it. We finally left the gift shop, and went outside. There was every type of business you would see in any Village, including, a General Store, Black Smith Shop, Barber Shop, Candle making Shop, Dress Shop, and a Livery Stable, to name a few. We spent most of the day there. If you ever travel through Bedford Pennsylvania I highly recommend that you take time to see the afore mentioned sights.

After spending two days in Bedford we got up the next morning, and headed for home. We had been gone twelve days, and we were ready to get back to the normal way of life. We drove down through the southern part of Pennsylvania, across the corner of West Virginia, crossed over into Virginia, and made our way back home to Farmville. The trip had taken us to places we had never been, and we had witnessed things that we had only read or heard about. It was a wonderful vacation, and we will never forget it. Sometimes, we reminisce about the vacation we took while we were living in Virginia. With the vacation behind us I had to get back to work. We got back home on Friday, and Saturday morning I went to the Jobsite to look at what had been done while we were gone. I could see that the contractors had made good progress during the two weeks I was gone. I was well pleased with the progress, but I was glad to get back to work, and start running the job myself.

Chapter 34

After getting back from our vacation we began looking around for other cities of interest including Burkeville, Lynchburg, and Richmond. Lela liked to go to Lynchburg to shop, but I couldn`t find my way in, and out of the city, I got lost every time I tried. Richmond was a nice city with bigger shopping malls, and there was monument avenue where you could see a different monument every block. Almost every time we were there we drove down monument Avenue. We found a nice Restaurant in an area called Shokco Slip. They had converted an old warehouse that was used to store, and ship tobacco, into a restaurant, and the food was great. We went there to eat almost every time we went to Richmond. The second ,and third floor was built from the four walls, extending out to an open space that reached from the first floor to the top of the building, with guard rails extending around the entire building. The space between the guard rail, and the back wall was used for dining areas, with stairways leading to each floor. this made for a great air space for dining. There were ropes that were threaded through pulleys that were anchored at the top of the building, making it possible to hoist trays of food up to each floor to be carried to the patrons that were dining on that floor.

The project at Hamden Sydney college moved along on or ahead of schedule with no apparent problems. Stan visited the jobsite every week or two. Each time he came we would walk over the site with me. Then as we walked up the hill he would say, everything looks good, keep it in the middle of the road. On one of his visits all he could talk about, was running. He had been introduced to the art of jogging, and he couldn`t stay off of the subject. He, my secretary, and myself went to lunch on campus. As we were coming back to the jobsite Stan said; drive down by the football field.! He said; I want to see you two run around the track, and I will see how long it takes. We did as he requested, and started running at a reasonable pace. we jogged about three quarters of the way around the track, and as he knew we would, we ran out of fuel, and walked the rest of the way. He met us at the finish line, shook our hands, and said; you both did good, better than I thought you would.

Stan had planted the seed, and it began to grow on me. If I walked anywhere I would jog part of the way. The more I walked the more I jogged, and before long I was jogging in the evening after work. Then Lela began jogging with me. We continued jogging in the evenings, ands week ends. Then I got word that the college was going to sponsor a ten K run from Hamden Sidney across the country to Farmville, and I signed up for it. I learned the route that the race would be run, and started training for the run, using that route. This would be my first race, and I wanted so much to do well. I practiced the run at least twice each week, until I knew where the up hills, and down hills were, and I tried to pace myself so I would have the energy to make it up the hills. The longest hill was toward the end of the race. I planed to run half way up the hill, and walk the other half. Then I would have a slight downhill run to the Longwood Girls College to the finish line.

On the day of the race I was at the starting line ready to go. The starter fired his gun, and the race was on. I ran the race just as I had several times before, but when I reached the last hill I didn`t make it half way, I only got one fourth of the way, and had to start walking. I kept going until I got my wind back, and started running again, when I topped the hill I thought I had it made now. When I got to where I could see the finish line I looked back and I didn`t see anyone, and I said; I must be the last one, but I looked back when I reached the finish line, and I could see others coming around the curve. That made me feel a much better. I continued running when I had time, but I didn`t do anymore ten K`s while I was in Virginia. When the field house was getting near completion Stan called me at my office, and started telling me that he would be leaving soon to move back to New York. I said; I thought you would never leave the south.! he said; I know I said that, but let me tell you the story. This Company contacted me three months ago, and I told them no, but they kept calling me every week, raising the amount they pay me, and they finally found my price. When will you go I asked? He said; it will be a while yet. I will bring my replacement with me the next time I come up. I think you will like him. He is a nice guy, and he will treat you as well as I have.

The next time he came to the jobsite he brought the man with him, and introduced him to me, and I don`t remember his name, but I will call him John, he did seem like a nice fellow. The field house was completed soon after John came aboard as my boss. When the Architect made his final inspection he noticed several leaks over the racket ball courts. I talked to the roof contractor, and asked him to come, and inspect the roof for possible leaks. I also asked the architect to come to the jobsite, and meet with us When they both arived at the jobsite we all went up on the roof. We inspected the roof area in question very closely, and couldn`t find anything that would cause a leak. Then we came down off of the roof, went up into the attic to look at the under side of the roof. At first we didn`t see anything, but after a closer inspection we noticed droplets of water hanging from the under side of the metal roof. I asked both of them what could cause that to happen? They both said; we don`t know. The architect said; let me do some research, and I will get back to you.

I called John, and told him what we had found, and told him that the architect was going to research the problem, and hopefully come up with a solution. He said; let me know what he comes up with. I want to come up there when he decides what has to be done to stop the water from dripping on the Racket ball courts. When I heard from the architect he told me he thought he had solved the problem, and he would contact John , and ask him to meet him at the Jobsite Friday morning at 10 A. M. When John arrived at my office I took him down to the field house, and showed him what we had found. He turned to me, and said; what do you think it is. I said; I`m not sure. We have two things to consider. The top side of the metal roof is cold, and the bottom side is warm. I think we may have a case of the moisture in the air is causing the droplets to form on the worm side of the metal. He said; you may be right.

When the architect arived we all went into my office, and sat down at the conference table. The architect said; Gentlemen I believe I have the solution. The moist air is migrating from the pool through the partition into the air space in the attic, and settling out on the bottom of the metal roofing in the form droplets of water. John looked at me with a slight smile on his face ,as if to say that's what you said. The architect unfolded a drawing, laid it on the table, and said; this should fix the problem. If we make this partition air tight it should stop the droplets from forming on the bottom of the metal roof. I said; I will see that this is done within the next seven days. Before John left he told me that he would talk to Bruce, and make arrangements for you to stay on the project until this problem is solved.

I called the architectural contractor, and asked him if he could come back immediately to do an extra for me on the Field house? I explained to him the nature of the work, and he said, I will be there Monday with a couple of men to do the job. He showed up Monday morning ready to work. I gave him the drawing, and told him to follow this drawing to the letter. When you are finished I will inspect the work, and sign your work order. By the end of the day Friday they had fished the job, and asked me to inspect it. I went down, and looked over it very carefully, and they had done a good job. I called the architect, and told him that everything was done according to the drawing. I inspected it carefully, and they did everything that you had marked on the drawings. He said; lets give it a week to dry off, and I will look at it next Friday. Then I called John, and told him what the architect said. He said; I will see you next Friday. In the meantime do whatever you have to do to pass the time. The next week dragged slowly by. I didn't have anything to do, but walk, and look. By the end of the week I was talking to myself.

Come Friday morning we all gathered in my office, and went down to the field house to take a look. We didn't have to look very long to see that nothing had changed. The water droplets were still clinging to the bottom of the roofing, and dripping on the hand ball courts. Back to the drawing board.! They kept me there checking every testing apparatus known to man. During that time I was there eight hours a day, five days a week making a log of what ever we were testing at the time. Finally after five months they still didn't have a solution to the problem. They decided I wouldn't be needed there after the end of the month. While all of this was going on we were making preparations to move back home. We made one last visit to the Country Club to say good bye to everyone, and we were amazed at the number of people who shook our hand, and wished us well.

Lela`s father had been sick for sometime, and we received a phone call that he had gotten worse. I took her to the Airport at Richmond, and sent her home to be with him. She had not been there long until he passed on. She called to tell me about it, and I told her that it would be difficult for me to come home for the funeral. We discussed it, and decided that I would stay there, and make arrangements to move home. In the meantime John had been trying to find a project to put me on. He called me one day and said; I have a project for you. But I don`t think you will want it. where is it I asked. He said; It`s in New York City. I said; you are right.! I don`t want it.! with that settled I called a moving Company, and made a deal with them to move me back to Benton Ark. I got a welding shop to build me a tow-bar for the front of my station wagon. I hooked it to the trailer hitch on my Lincoln Mark Four, and pulled it to my apartment, and unhooked it.

The movers arived early the next morning, and had it all loaded by nine o-clock, and drove away with it. After the movers left I went over to Farmville , and ate breakfast in a restaurant there in town. Then I drove back to the apartment, and loaded everything else into the station wagon, cleaned the apartment, went to the office, gave Bruce the keys to the apartment, and said good bye to the people in the office. When I got back to the apartment I hooked the station wagon to the car, put ginger in the back seat, and drove off with a feeling that part of me didn`t want to go. After all I had been there two years working with these people, and I knew I was going to miss them. I drove slowly out to the highway, turned right, and headed down the highway toward Keysville. As I drove down the road I couldn`t help, but think, I will never be treated better than I have been in Hamden Sydney. and Farmville. Virginia. I took it easy for a while for I had not towed a car before, but it didn`t take long to get used to it.

We stopped at Roanoke Virginia, and stayed the night, got up early the net morning, and drove about 200 miles before eating breakfast. I gave ginger her food before I went into the Restaurant. When I finished eating I went out to the car to let ginger out to do her thing. She hurried back to the car, hopped in, laid down on her blanket, looked at me as if to say , am ready to go. I drove out of on the highway and we were on our way again. I drove along at a steady pace, stopping only when we both needed to go top the bath room. Then we were back on the Freeway headed for home. We made it to Memphis before the sun went down, and stayed in a hotel there. We were up early the next morning, had our breakfast at the Hotel, and got on the Freeway loop out of town heading for Benton Arkansas. The traffic was light, and we got home about ten 0-c lock in the morning. I had called Lela from Memphis, and told her when I thought I would be there, and she was there waiting for us at the little house when we got there. The people had not moved out of the big house. We had to move into the little house.

Chapter 35

The moving van came the next day, we unloaded all that would go into the little house, and stored the rest in their warehouse in Little Rock. We had the power, and telephone turned on, and lived there until the people moved out of the big house. Then we moved into the big house, and had the furniture that was in storage brought down to us. I hadn`t been back more than a couple of days when Ralph came to see me, and asked me if I wanted to help him on his repair work? I said; yes I can do that.! Of course if I get called back to work I will have to go. He said; that`s understood.! I worked with him until late in the year, when I got a job with Blunt Construction Co. in Mobile Alabama. They needed me on a project they were doing for I. B. M. in Charlotte North Carolina. They wanted me to be there the first week in Jan. l left home to go to Charlotte the second day of Jan. I got to the jobsite about noon Jan 3 rd. The project manager told me go find a motel room, and come back in the morning. I went back the next morning, went into his office. We talked a few minutes, and walked down to the building area.

He took me to an area where they were starting the foundation for a new building, and   said, "This is your building! I have another building I want you to look after until it is finished." We walked back up a long flight of steps to the office complex. He took me in and showed me my office. There was a plan table with plans laid out on it, with everything I needed to work with. He told me to take some time to get acquainted with the staff, and the building area. He also told me to spend some time each day looking for a place to live. Then he took me outside to a truck, and said; this is your truck. You can use it for everything pertaining to the job, but you can`t use it for your personal use. I stayed on the jobsite until after lunch, and went to a motel to secure a room. I spent the first week getting more acquainted with the job, and hunting a place to live, which was no easy task.

During the week end I bought a Newspaper, and started looking at the rental adds. I found one that seemed to be just what I wanted. I called the number that was listed, and told the guy I was interested in renting the house that he had listed in the paper. He told me he could show me the house at 28212 Saddle Horse Lane Monday evening after five o 0- clock. I told him I would meet him at that Address at the specified time. When I left the job on Monday afternoon I drove to the Address on Saddle Horse Lane, and looked at the house inside, and outside. I said; how much is the rent? He told me the rental amount, and I said; I will take it. He asked when I would want to move in? I told him I would like to occupy the house the first of next week. He said; that will be fine. I will start your payment period next Monday.

I called Lela, and told her I had found a house, and suggested that she call a mover in Little Rock. She called me back, and told me the movers could have everything packed, and ready to load Saturday morning. I told my Boss my plan, and he said; that will work. Why don`t you plan to start home Thursday so you will be there when they come the load the van. I got home Friday afternoon, spent the night there, and was ready for the movers Saturday morning. When the van was loaded they said, we will see you in Charlotte Monday morning. We went by Lela`s mothers house, visited with her a while, and headed for Charlotte north Carolina. We arived in Charlotte Sunday evening, spent the night in a motel, and was there when the moving van arived. It was almost noon when the movers finished unloading ,and setting up the furniture in the proper rooms.

While we were at Hardy Arkansas we took some dancing lessons, and began to enjoy going to civic centers to round dance, where the refreshments were limited to coffee, and cold drinks. Soon after we arived in Charlotte we began looking in the News Papers for advertisements of a place we could go. Lela found an advertisement in the paper about a place on Lake Norman. They met every Saturday night from 8 0-clock to 10 0-clock. It sounded like what we were looking for. We drove up there to see what it looked like. We had a little trouble finding the place, but after stopping at a service station they told us how to get there. We walked inside, stopped, looked around. A couple sitting at a table, got up, walked up to us, and said; would you like to sit with us? we said , yes we would. We sat down at their table. That is how we met

Walter, and Rachel Little. They lived on the family farm where Walter grew up. We visited with them in their home, and they visited in our home, and they became as good of friends as we have ever had.

We learned a lot about Charlotte by driving around looking at things that we had not seen before. We also took drives in the country just to see what was there. We went to our first pro golf tournament at Quail Hollow, and saw Arnold Palmer, Jack Nickelous, and Lee Treveno, just to name a few. They didn't kook as big as they did on T. V. We enjoyed walking around the course watching them play golf. They played a completely different kind of golf than me, and my buddies, but we had fun playing our kind of golf. Sometimes Lela, and I played by ourselves, and enjoyed it very much. Another thing we really enjoyed was the car races at the Charlotte Speedway. The first couple that we met after moving there was [John, and Shirley] their son won four tickets to the races. He gave the tickets to them, and they invited us to go to the races with them in their Buick convertible. Our seats were half way between the stating platform, and the first turn. When the starter dropped the checkered flag the cars came roaring by us into the first turn, and I know my hair stood strait up on my head. It was the thrill of my life.

While we were at Charlotte, my mother passed away, and we went to her funeral. after the service we were at my sisters house discussing what to do with all of her belongings Our older brother suggested that we start having a family Reunion each year, starting the following year which would be 1982 We decided to lock her house up, and have the first reunion at her house some time in June. We would lay everything out where it could be seen, and each of us could put our name on what we wanted. If more than one name was on an item, we would draw straws for it, and we all agreed, that because Lois our youngest sister had lived next door to our mother, and took care of her, had first choice of anything that she wanted. We also agreed that whoever had the reunion at their house, could choose the week end in June to have it. At this point in time we have met for the Reunion 26 times, and the next, will be at Branson Missouri hosted by Ron, and Lora Morgan.

After I was there one year, there was a reduction in the workforce, and Guess what? All of the others had more time with the Company than I did, and I was laid off. The Project Manager said; we will move you back home. I told him that we liked it here, and asked him if he would give me the money that it would cost to move us home, so I could stay here, and look for a job, and if I couldn't get a job I could use the money to move myself back home. He thought about it for a minute, and said; yes I can do that. I sent my resume to at least a dozen Contractors, and did not get a response from any one of them. Then I called a man I had worked for before, and told him that I had been laid off. He told me he would hire me if he had an opening for someone like me. Let me check around to see if I can find a project to put you on He called back later, and told me he didn't have a thing that he could use me on. Lela, and I discussed our situation, and decided we couldn't stay there any longer without a job.

Chapter 36

We called a moving Company, and made a deal with them to pack our things, load the van, and allow me to drive it home, They came the next day to pack everything, and the next day they were there early to load the van. When the van was about loaded some of our neighbors came over to help us with the last minute items that is usually left behind, and told us they had enjoyed having us for a neighbor. They also helped us look around the house one last time to be sure we didn`t forget anything. With that done we all shook hands, hugged, said, good bye, and we will miss you all. Then I put ginger in the truck, climbed in with her, drove out to the street with Lela following behind, and waved again as we drove away. It is very difficult to leave good friends behind after being neighbors for a year. As we pulled out on the street that would take us to the highway we had an uneasy feeling that we were leaving something behind, but we can always look back to the time when we lived on Saddle Horse Lane. in Charlotte North Carolina

We got as far as Cookeville Tennessee the first day, got a room in a nice Motel. We were up early the next morning, ate breakfast, and was on our way to Benton Arkansas. We made good time even though I couldn`t get much over 60 miles per hour out of the moving van. We only stopped when we needed to use the bathroom. It certainly didn`t take ginger long to relieve herself. If we stopped on the roadside, and opened the door she hit the ground squatting, in a matter of seconds she would be back in the truck ready to go. In those days we traveled enough to know the best way to get where we were going was to keep peddling as fast as you could, and never spend more than five minutes at a rest stop. We kept peddling as fast as we could, and stopping five minutes at a time, unless we had more than one reason to stop. By using that method we were able to get to 1110 Henry street in Benton by mid afternoon. We called the moving company, and asked them to send a crew down to unload the van. We spent the night with James, and Debbie. We went back to our house the next morning to meet the unloading crew. When that was done they took the moving van back with them.

After they left we still had plenty work to do, such as putting all the things in boxes under the bed, and putting the clothes in the closets. Then there was the outside work that needed to be done. It was always grown up when we came back after being gone for a while. I spent most of my time the first week cleaning up the yard, trimming the bushes, and the scrubs I hadn't been home more than a week when Ralph came over to my house, and asked me if I could help him. He always had more work than he could say grace over. I appreciated it because I always needed something to do to make dollar or two, and that is the nature of construction. No matter how good you are at what you do you will be out of work now, and then. If you work for a big Company you better be ready to travel. That's why I have worked all over the country. If you don't stay with them they want stay with you.

Lela, and I were privileged to be associated with more than one contractor that would move us from one place to another. That gave us an opportunity to meet and become friends with people all across the country. Some of our friends at home would say to us, we sure wouldn't want to do what you two are doing, and we would say to them. We are having a ball. We are more or less being forced into situations where we are meeting new people, learning, their ways, and becoming friends with people we would never have met any other way. We learned, that just because people live in another state, and do things a little different than we do, doesn't mean that they are bad people, or mean people. We made a lot of friends across the country. Some were better than others but we called them all, friends. We wouldn't take anything for the friends that we made moving around from one state to another. We say, if you need a friend, be a friend.

Chapter 37

I continued working with Ralph, and looking for job until July. Then I received a call from Ed Cailouette in San Francisco asking me if I would be interested in coming out there to do a job. I asked him, how long will the job take? He said; at least six mouths, and went on to say he would try to keep me longer if other projects became available. He asked me to send him a letter telling him how much it would take to get me out there. I composed a letter listing all the things that I could think of, and being careful not to miss anything. I went back over it, padding every item to the fullest, hoping it would be more than he would be willing to pay. He called me back, told me he had read my letter, and in addition to what I had listed, he would pay me a 38 % side adder. to cover house rental, and other miscellaneous items. Then he said; when can you be here? I wasn`t ready for that. When I regained my composure I said; in a week. I need to tie up some loose ends first. He said; that sounds like a winner. I will send you and Lela both a plane ticket to San Francisco, and you can fly out as soon as possible.

I got busy getting everything wrapped up to a point that it would be alright for us to go to San Francisco, and when the plane tickets arived there was a message from Ed, saying why don`t you fly out here Friday, and take tour of San Francisco Saturday. Then you could take it easy Sunday. Then I will meet you at the motel Monday morning for breakfast. Friday morning we went to the Little rock airport, and caught a plane to San Francisco. When we arived at the San Francisco International Airport we got on a shuttle bus that took us to the Holiday Inn in South San Francisco. We got off the shuttle, went inside, and checked in. the lady at the counter gave us the keys to our room, and told us that a tour bus to San Francisco would be leaving at 8 O- clock the next morning. We were up Saturday morning, had our breakfast, and caught the tour bus to San Francisco.

We had never been to San Francisco, and you can imagine our surprise when the bus drove by a gay parade. We simply could not believe our eyes, but there it was for the world to see. The bus drove all over the city showing us the sights, including the Golden Gate Bridge, Golden Gate Park ,Fisherman's Warf, Coit Tower, and the Museum of Modern Art. I immediately liked San Francisco. We made it a monthly thing to do. When you get near the city on highway101 you will turn slightly to the left as you go over the top of the hill, and suddenly you have a panoramic view of the whole city. You have to see it yourself to understand the impact it has on you. The tour used up most of the day, and we enjoyed everything that we saw. It was nice to get back to the Motel, relax, and talk about all the things we had seen that day.

We got up late Sunday morning, made some coffee in the room, sipped on it while we watched T. V. then had a late breakfast in the motel breakfast room. Then we went back to our room, and layed around watching T. V. until late in the afternoon Then we got up, cleaned up a bit, went down to the dining room, and had dinner. After dinner we went into the lounge, sat down in a couple of lounge chairs, and watched people coming, in, and going out of the dining room until it ceased to be amusing anymore, and went back to our room, put on our sleeping clothes, and went to bed. Monday morning we were up fairly early, bathed, dressed and went down to the breakfast room. When we walked in, Ed was already there at a table. He got up, shook our hands, and said; it's good to see you two. We sat back down, and talked about the job as we ate breakfast. When we finished eating we went out, got in his car, and drove up to South San Francisco where they were working on a new Research, and development building for Genentect Inc. He took us in, and introduced us to some of the people in the office. Then he drove down a street between two rows of buildings, and stopped. This is your job.

That is an empty building. You will be transforming that empty space into a number of Research, and Development Laboratories. They will be similar to those you built in Cleveland Mssissippi at the Baxter Travenol plant. Then he took us to the San Francisco international airport, and picked up a rental car that he had reserved for me. Then he said; follow me! He drove out to the freeway, took the ramp that would put us on Highway 101southbound. I followed him as closely as possible. I wasn't used to driving on an eight lane Freeway, but I stayed close enough to follow him off the Freeway, took a left turn under the Freeway, into Foster City. He drove into the first parking area , and parked. I parked beside him. He told me to get in the car with him, and Lela. Then he showed us where several of the Fluor Daniel people lived. He then showed us where he, and his wife Maryland lived. Then he showed us where others lived all over Foster City. Then he took us back to the parking lot where I parked the rental car. Then he told me to use the rental car until you find place to rent, and stay at the Holiday Inn until you are ready to go back home, and move your household, and your cars out here.

Ed gave us the name of a Realestate Company that had helped some of the others find a place to rent. The next day we went to see them, and a lady drove all over Foster City looking at houses, and found one late in the evening at 371 Boothbay in Foster City. After looking through the house we told her we would take. I called Ed, and told him that we had found a house that we could a occupy immediately. He said; that sounds good. I'll get you a roundtrip ticket, and make arrangements with a moving company to come to your house, and start packing as soon as you get home to call them. The airline ticket will be waiting for you at at the ticket counter at United Air Lines. Let me know when you will be getting back to San Francisco? We got up early the next morning, got dressed, went down to the breakfast room, ate breakfast, checked out of the Motel, drove to the Airport, went to the desk, picked up our tickets, and waited to board the plane to Little rock Ark. While we were waiting for the plane to take off we called Debbie, and told her when we would arrive at Little rock.

It was a beautiful day to fly, and we enjoyed the trip. We made good time to Dallas, but we had to change planes there, and had a short lay over. Once we were on the plane to Little Rock, it didn't take long to get there. When we got off the plane, Debbie was right there to pick us up. We went down to the baggage department, picked up our lugged, carried it out to the car and we were on our way home. As soon as we got home we called the movers, and told them we were ready for them to come to the house, and pack our things. they were there early the next morning. By the end of the day they had everything packed, and ready to be loaded into the van. The van was there the next morning ready to start loading. They put the furniture, and the other household items in the front of the van. Then they put our Mark four Lincoln in the back of the van. We gave the driver our Address in Foster City. Just before leaving he said, I will see you Sunday afternoon at 371 Boothbay in Foster City Ca. He drove away from the house about 12:00- 0 -clock Friday. Soon after he left, a car transport picked up our Ford station Wagon, and drove off with it. We spent the night with James,and Debbie, and our two grand daughters, Jill & Julie.

We caught a plane Sunday morning that would get us to San Francisco about mid afternoon, and on arrival we went to the Holiday Inn to spend the night. We checked out of the motel about 11; 00 o clock, and went to the a grocery store, bought some groceries. Then went to the house we had rented, and put the groceries in the cabinets, and waited for the van to get there. We hadn`t been there long when the Van pulled up in front of the house, They unloaded the car first, and started unloading the household items. It was dark when they got it all in the house. Then they started assembling the furniture, and putting it in place. When they finlly got it all in place it was almost midnight. The driver kept asking, If there was anything else he could help us with. We kept telling him no. there is nothing more you can do. I thought we would never get him out of the house so we could go to bed, but he finally left, and we were able to get to bed a little after midnight.

Even though we got to bed late we were up early enough for me to go to work. When I got to the jobsite I went into the main office, and talked to Ed, a few minutes, and he went with me to my new project. On the way over there he told me there was a Datsun truck I could use until he could find one better. We looked at the plans together, to see how the architect had designed the project, in an effort to followed his plans as near as possible. Ed told me he had Tom smith coming out from Greenville to work with me on an equal basis. I said; that want work. He said; why want it work? I answered, and said, a project can only have one Boss. Then you are it. Later in the week I got a message to meet the car transport driver at a parking area in Foster City to get my Station Wagon.

Chapter 38

I began calling each contractor as they were needed, to begin the work, that they had contracted to do, with each craft having a small time period between them, and the craft before, or after them. This should eliminate the possibility of any conflict between the various contractors. This method worked very well. I had no complaints from any contractor about somebody being in his way. Tom Smith, and I worked well together. He worked with the contracts, and work orders, and I ran the overall project. We kept on schedule except for extended time for work orders, and the project finished on schedule. While this was going on, Lela, and I had the opportunity to go to San Francisco, and look around. We found some very interesting places besides the ones we saw on the bus tour the first day we were there. We always went to the fisherman`s wharf every time we were in the City. We also had to go ghiradelli square, and get some of their chocolates. And of course we always enjoyed seeing the black man on the corner with his guitar, making up cute little songs about the ladies as they walked by.

We had only been in the house at 371 Boothbay a short time when the door bell rang one evening. I went to the door, and there stood a man, and a woman. The man said, I am George Barnes, and this is my wife Libby. We are from the Western Hills Baptist Church. In San Mateo, and we would like to invite you to our services Sunday morning. We asked them in, and they told us how to get there, and we told them we would be there. We went to the morning service, and enjoyed it, and continued to worship there as long as we were in California. About half of the congregation was from some of the southern States. That was probably one of the reasons we felt comfortable there. The first Sunday we went to Western Hills Baptist church, a lady walked over to Lela, and said, i`m Ann Adams, and I am very pleased to meet you. As they talked she asked Lela if she walked, and Lela said; yes I do. Would you like to walk with me? Lela said; yes I think I would Where do you live she asked? Lela gave her our Address, and she showed up at our house the next morning. They walked together, and became very good friends. Ann owned a Western store in San Bruno, Before long Lela was working for Ann in the Western store, and every time we went back out there she would work at store with Ann, and we also went back to the Western Hills Baptist church.

In the following spring we began seeing advertisements in the Newspaper about a Bay to breaker run, that always took place in May. I asked Ed about it, and he said, yes. there is a run from the Bay, across to the city to the ocean, called the Bay to breakers. You should sign up for that run." I said,"I doubt if I am in shape for that. He said, "why don`t you run it with Maryland. She can`t run it all the way without waking. I would like to have someone like you with her to take care of her in case of an injury. "I said; I`ll do that. When the day arived we all got together, drove up close to the finish line, parked our cars, and carpool to the starting line, and drop off the runners. Then we would wait for the starting gun. sometimes we had to wait as much as an hour. Maryland , and I got in the back of the line. When the starting gun fired, everybody took off, except us. We had to wait for all the others to get out of the way before we could start. it was at least 15 minutes before we crossed the start line. We made it pretty well until we got. to Hayes Hill. Then we had to walk all the way up to the top. Then we had it down grade, and up grade for about a mile, and after that it was down grade all the way to the Breakers.

Chapter 39

After the first job was complete I was placed on a project as Construction Manager for Bio-Response inc. at Hayward California, Responsible for construction management on the interior improvements on a sophisticated genetic engineering facility. The Project received very favorable reviews from the owner, and made the local Newspapers. At this point in time the Datsun truck I was driving was about worn out. Ed told me to look around to see what I could find to lease for me to drive. I called a Chevrolet dealer, and told them what I needed. He said; I have just the truck for you. It is an S. 10 Chevy, with extended cab, and large mirrors. I can give you a three year lease with a maximum of 15,000 miles per year with a buyout price of $5,000. I gave him Ed`s phone number, and told him to talk to him about it. Ed called me later, and said, come by, and get your new truck. This truck became known as a Cadillac truck, after, Jim Durham referred to it as Rays Cadillac truck.

When I first got to California Ed began inviting me to play golf with him in the evening after work, and on Saturdays. Then I learned that Fluor Daniel had a Company Tournament each month, and I began playing in the tournament. We would drive as far as 100 miles to play in the Company Tournament. Soon after that Jim Willey, and I teamed up with two guys from the fluor side of the company, and played as a foursome each Saturday. We did that as long as I was in California, but we never played the same course two times in succession. I intended to make a list of all the different courses we played on, but I didn`t get around to it. I suppose we all have had a few things that we intended to do, but just never got around to doing them. If we always did the things that we intended to do, our life story might have been entirely different.

On my next Project I was Construction Superintendent, for Genencor, a subsidiary of Genentect Inc. at south San Francisco,

California. Responsible for all phases of construction of enzyme research Labs, and Offices. While I was working that job my youngest daughter, Debbie Tully, her Husband James, and their to daughters, Jill, and Julie, flew out to spend a week with us. James had not flown before, and it took the whole family a while to talk him into getting on the plane. James is a fisherman, and he wanted to go deep sea fishing, and they enjoyed it very much, except when they were seasick. Then we took them to San Francisco to see the sights, including Fisherman Wharf. Then we took them down the Crookedest street in the world.

.When the genentcor Project was finished I was sent to Palo Alto California as the Construction Manager, for Alza Corporation, Responsible for directing, monitoring, and controlling subcontractors, activities on a Library, and Cafeteria grass roots addition using all open-shop subcontractors. This Project turned out to be a new experience. The local Union picketed the project. There was a fence at the entrance to the jobsite, with two gates. We were advised by Fluor Daniel that the Union could only picket one gate, and all of the workers could enter through the other gate. They sat there on that gate for weeks, calling us all sorts of lovely names, but we did not respond to anything they said to us. Of course their being there had its effect on the progress of the project, but we all worked hard to overcome the time delay, and the project was completed in a timely manner, without Excessive cost to the owners.

Ed told me he didn`t have a project to put me on, but he needed me to go to the Jelly Belly project in Fairfield, and help the superintendent on that project. I went to Fairfield the following morning. I got there about 9 0-clock, met with the superintendent. He showed me around the project, took me to the office, and introduced me to the President of the Jelly Belly Company. The president was a big man, at least a head taller than me, and a very likeable man. He started talking to me like he had always known me, gave me a lapel pen, and gave me some Jelly Beans samples to take with me. Then he said, we always have samples here for the taking.

When I went up there the following Monday morning there was a picket on the front gate. they must have known that I was coming. Since I had the experience at Alza, Jim Wiley told me to work with the Union on that Project as well. They called us a lot of ugly names, but

I was used to that. They sat out there a couple of weeks, then got up, and left, and we were non the worse for them being there. I worked with the Jelly Belly project for approximately two, and a half mouths I would drive up Monday morning, stay at a motel Monday, and Tuesday night, drive home Wednesday evening, and drive back to the job Thursday morning, stay in a motel Thursday night, and drive home Friday evening, spend the week end at home in San Mateo, and do the same the next week. I signed up for the Bay to Breakers in May of 1984, but I ran it that time, and it was a whole different experience. I got as close to the starting line as I could. When the starting gun fired, I started running, and I found that I was surrounded by people completely unlike those in my first run. I saw runners pushing baby buggies, pulling babies in wagons, and caring their kids piggy back. There were several centipedes of all variations, and there was every type of dress, and undress, than you could imagine, and a few nudes.

In June of 1985 our oldest daughter Diane, and her three suns, Chris. Paul, and Jon drove out to visit. They stayed with us until mid August, and we had more fun that summer than you would believe. We took them to Fisherman Wharf, and while we were there the boys wanted to go over to Alcatraz. We also took them to other places including the Winchester House, In San Hose, the Muir woods, and my favorite running trail just off I-280. I usually ran there three evenings a week. When we would leave the starting line, Jon would take off as fat as he could, run to the two mile marker, and wait for us. When we caught up with him, we would go on to the three mile marker, and turn back. On the way back Jon was always the last to get to where we started. San Mateo sponsored a 7 K run while they there, and we all entered the race. When the starting gun sounded Jon took off like a Deer, being chased by a dog. Then Paul, Chris, myself, Diane, and Lela. Somewhere along the trail John faltered, Chris, Paul, and I passed him, and through some kind of Miracle I was there to greet them at the finish line.[THAT] made my day.

Chapter 40

My next project was at South San Francisco. As Construction superintendent, Responsible for directing, monitoring, and controlling the Civil, Structural, and Architectural contractors for constructing the Lab Block # 4 Project for Genentect Inc, and maintaining the Safety :Program. The Project started August I 1985, and finished on July 11 1986,and I was put on an availability leave of absence until they could find a project to put me on. I began making arrangements to move back to Benton. Ed told me that the company would pay the expense to move me back home, but I would have to drive the van. I rented the biggest van that Rider had, and paid a crew to pack, and load the van. I had purchased the[Cadillac] truck for the residual value, and rented a bumper hitch to pull it behind the van. I shipped our car to a nearby city in ark. When we got everything ready we put ginger behind the seat, climbed up into the van, and drove away. I was a little uneasy driving a 38 foot van, towing a S 10 pick up truck, but I remembered driving a dump truck when I was a young man, and that made me feel more at ease. God is good, and god forgives. There was a time in my life that I strayed away from god, and did some things I shouldn`t have done. I also sinned against my wife. They both have forgiven me, and I love them dearly for it. I have become much closer to God, and my Wife since that time.

It took four days to drive home. The van had a governor on it, and wouldn`t go more than 60 miles per hour down hill. When I got to those long grades, it would be down to 25 miles per hour when I went over the top of the mountain. I learned something that most truck drivers probably learned on their first run. If you are going down hill, and see another hill in front of you, keep all the speed you are legally allowed, and, make a run for it, and you will get farther up the hill before you loose all of your momentum. We got up early each day, had an early breakfast, and drove all day until late in the evening. On the second evening we were getting near Albuquerque New Mexico when we decided to get a Motel room, and spend the night there. I steered the van off the freeway on to the service road, took a right turn at the first intersection, took another right on to a four lane street, and because of my length moved over to the second lane when I got near a motel driveway I turned my right turn signal on, checked the rear view mirror, and turned into the driveway. Halfway into the turn I heard the screeching of tires, and by the time I could get my truck off the street I knew I had hit something. I stopped, got out, went around to the other side of the van, and there was a Nissan 280 Z pinned under the van in front of the duel wheels.

I went into the motel and asked them to call the police. Before the police came the driver of the 280 Z made a telephone call. In a very short time a car drove in close to the truck took a box out of the 280 Z put it in the other car, and drove off down the street with it before the police got there. When they arived I explained to them what had happened, and witnesses verified what I had told them, they told me to go ahead, and spend the night in the Motel, but I needed to come to the police Department, and fill out a report before I left the city. We got up the next morning, ate breakfast gassed up the truck, drove three miles back to city hall, filled out the report, and got on 1 40 going east. We lost about an hour before we left the city. We drove a little later in the evening before we stopped, trying to gain back some of the time we had lost that morning. We spent the night in a small town in Oklahoma. The next day we got to Ozark Arkansas, and spent the night there. We were up early the next the morning, ate breakfast, and got on the road early. We got to Benton before noon, and drove straight to 1901 Harmon drive, where we would be living for I while.

We had stopped at a service station, and called the moving company to come down, and unload the van. They got to the house a short time after we did, and had the van unloaded by six o- clock. We had bought the house on one of our trips home, and had leased it to a family until we knew that we were coming home to live in it ourselves. We were anxious to spend the first night in it. It took a couple of days to get everything placed where we wanted it, or where we could live with it. When Ralph learned that we were home he came over, and as usual asked me if I would help him while I was waiting for Fluor Daniel to call me to do another project for them. I told him I would be glad to help him. We had not been home very long when Doyle & Billie Wilson came to see us, and asked us to take lessons to learn to Square Dance We said yes, we would try it for a while. We attended a few lessons, and began to enjoy it. We continued Square Dancing as long as we were in Benton. I worked with Ralph for more than a year.

Chapter 41

Then Fluor Daniel Inc. called, and said, they needed me to do another project for Genentect Inc as Construction Superintendent: Responsible for directing, monitoring, and controlling, Civil, Structural, and Architectural Contractors for construction of a TPA packaging, and shipping facility, and maintaining the Safety Program. While I was in California looking for a place to live, Lela called, and told me that it had snowed, and Ginger was lost in the snow, and she had not been able to find her. Two days later she called, and told me that she found Ginger in the back yard. She was in bad shape, and she had taken her to the Vet. After his examination he told her that her condition was so bad, that the only humane thing to do was to put her to sleep. She told him go ahead with it, but I don`t want to know when it happens.

In January 1988 we moved back to San Mateo California at 1209 West Hillsdale Blvd, to build the project mentioned above. We didn`t take as much of our belongings as we did when we went to California the first time. We sent only enough in the moving van to have an extra bedroom, and put the rest in our truck, and car. We rented a Dollie, and pulled the car behind the truck. Everything went well until we got out in Arizona. We spent the night in Winslow, got up early, and started up the long grade toward Flagstaff. When we reached the higher elevations, we began to see snow.

The snow got deeper with every mile, and before we reached the city limits we were driving over the roughest surface I have seen in a long time. Apparently the snow had thawed the day before, and froze again during the night, leaving all the ruts from the day before. We drove through the city at about twenty miles per hour. When we reached the top of a hill it was doubtful that we would climb the next hill, but we kept moving over one hill after another until we started back down hill, and the snow began to melt. Soon we got below the snow line, and began to pick up speed again. What a relief, that was good to get behind us. That was the only problem we had on the entire trip. When we arived at the apartment, we unloaded what we had brought in the truck, and car. Then we started thinking about what we would sleep on until our furniture arived. I got the air mattress out of the bag, and began to pump it up, only to find that the foot pump would not work.

I got in the car, drove down to a parts store, bought a hand pump, brought it back, and pumped up the mattress. With that done we hooked up a portable T. V. we had brought with us to watch until bed time, but we had no chairs to sit on. We sat on the floor, and leaned against the wall, it didn`t take long for us to realize that we were not wall leaners. We laid down on the air mattress, and managed to sleep [some] before morning. I got up the next morning, reported to work, and met the man that I would be responsible to. He took me out into an existing building, and showed me what we were in the process of changing the room layout to suit Genentects need for a TPA packaging, and Shipping Facility. Then he took me back to the office, and showed me the plans, and the schedule. He said, you can spend some time looking at the plans, and schedule, and see what we are trying to do here . I looked at them the remainder of the day. The plans tell me how we are going to do each item of work, and the schedule tells me when it has to be started, and when it has to be finished. That is how I always manage a project. If any craft fell behind the schedule I was there to see that they got back on schedule even if it meant increasing their manpower. I was there in may, when the Bay to breakers took place, and I entered the race. I didn`t break any records, but I finished the race.

While we lived on Hillsdale Blvd we met Irma from El Salvador. She lived down stairs with her son. She was a small woman with a big smile, and always seemed to be happy. Lela invited her to walk with her, and she came out of her apartment wearing rubber boots. Lela didn`t say anything at the time, but Irma complained about them hurting her feet later. Lela told her that she needed something lighter, and the next time she came out with her house shoes on. That didn`t work either. She finely bought a pair of athletic shoes. She invited us to dinner one evening in her apartment. When we got to her apartment she had everything decorated fit for a king, and queen. She poured us a drink out of a pitcher for us to drink while she finished getting everything ready. I didn't know what was in the drink, but it tasted pretty good. We had no idea what she had fixed for us to eat but it tasted wonderful, and we enjoyed it, and her very much. She was a wonderful hostess.

That project lasted until October of 1988, I must have done my job well. They told me that I had done a good job, but my part of the job was finished, and they didn't have another job to put ne on, and they said they would pay our expenses to move back home. We will get in touch with you if we get a project to put you on .We shipped the big things home, and hauled the rest in the car, and truck. We purchased a pair of Walkie Talkies. I drove the truck, and Lela followed me in the car. That way we could communicate with each other. I had ginger in the truck with me, and Lela had her Walkie Talkie so she could let me know when she needed to stop for any reason, and she could also tell me where to park. if I couldn't find a place.

We only had two meals a day. Breakfast, and dinner. We bought an assortment of things we could snack on through the day, and plenty water to drink with it, and left both within arms reach. The only time we stopped for was gas, or go to the bathroom, Or both. We drove along I -40 eating, and drinking. We made better time by driving through the lunch hour each day, and at the end of the third day we were only about 100 miles from home. We were dirty, tired, and in need of a bath. We stopped at Russelville, got a motel room, and spent the night. We were up early the next morning, had breakfast, and headed down the Freeway toward Benton. We arived at Lela's Mother, and Fathers house About 9-oclock in the morning, and called the moving co, and told them that we would let them know where to deliver the furniture that they had brought from California.

We looked around for a place to live, and rented a small house from Doyle & Bill Wilson at 3201Congo Road across the Road from where they lived. The Star Prominaders Square Dance club was starting lessons, and they asked us to help train the new members. The lessons were being taught in Doyle's shop near the house that we lived in. All we had to do was walk out the back door, walk over to the shop, and we were there ready to go. In addition to that we danced at Bauxite on Friday night. As usual I helped Ralph with his house repair Business while I waited for a call from Fluor Daniel asking me to come back, and do another project for them in California. I didn't have to wait long.

Chapter 42

Early in January 1989 they called me , and asked me if I would come back to California, and help with a project in San Hose with the same responsibilities as I had in other projects before, and especially in maintaining the Safety Program. I said; yes I will! They said there will be an airline ticket at the American Airlines counter in little rock Arkansas for you to pick up as soon as you can. I picked up the airline ticket the next morning and boarded the plane to Sans Francisco. I arived in San Francisco about 3-0 clock in the afternoon, and was met at the Airport by Ralph Brown. He took me to the car rental place where I picked up a rental car that they had reserved for me. He said, follow me, and I will show you where the Motel is that you will be staying in until you find a place to live. Then we went to the jobsite in San Hose and met with Jerald Norman, the General Superintendent of the Project. He walked us through the jobsite showing us the work in progress, and what was to be started next. I had already met Jerald when I first came to California.

Gerald said; I am glad to have you aboard! With your expertise in Civil, Structural , and Architectural, I believe we can move the project along faster than we have before. I said; I`ll do my best. I went to work the next morning ready to get things moving to a point of getting back on schedule. Gerald, and I reviewed the schedule, and the plans to reveal the most critical areas to concentrate on. With this information I began to talk to the contractors that was holding up the progress, and was able to plant some ideas in their mind that would bring the C.S.A contracts back in line with the schedule in a short time. In the mean time I was looking for a place to live. Each evening I would get the News Paper, and look for apartments to rent. If one sounded good I would go look at it. I kept doing that until one day I called about an apartment at 2811 Flores st in San Mateo. The lady described what she had available, and I went to look at it. When I walked into the apartment I knew that it was what I was looking for. I told her I would take it, and paid her the first months rent including the security.

I told Gerald I had found an apartment, and needed to fly home to move my furniture out to California. He said; go ahead, but hurry back. I got an early flight the next morning, and started getting things together for the trip. We went Square Dancing Friday night with our friends, and said our good byes. I got up Saturday morning, went to Little Rock, picked up a 5 feet x 8 feet trailer at U- haul Co, and brought it home, and started loading it. I had made a diagram, showing where everything should go in the trailer. We loaded it according to the diagram, and it worked out like I had planned. The last piece that was put in the trailer was a broom., and there was no more room for anything bigger than a broom handle.

We got everything loaded about one 0-clock, said good bye to Doyle & Billie , and hit the road for California. We had made so many trips back, and forth that we knew where all the good places were to spend the night. We drove until after dark, and stopped at one of our favorite places to spend the night. After a good nights sleep we were on the road again headed west. It took almost four days to get to get to our apartment in San Mateo. We called the Western Hills Baptist Church, and asked if there was anyone there that could help us unload our furniture. In about thirty minutes two men drove up , and said, we are here to help you unload. With their help we had everything unloaded, and moved into the third floor apartment in about an hour.

We told them we appreciated their help so very much, and we could handle it from here on. After they left we got busy putting everything in it's place, and before long we had everything put away, and out if sight to a point that we could sit down ,and rest a while. We later moved things around a bit to get them in a more suitable place. I was there when the bay to breaker race was run that year, and I entered it for the sixth, and last time. I made the best time I had ever had before. I crossed the finish line in one hour, and sixteen minutes. I received a letter saying that I came in within the first sixteen thousand,--but there was 100,000 people in the race.

I called Gerald, and told him I would be back to work the next morning. I went to work the next morning ready to renew my effort to bring the C.S.A Contractors back on schedule. They had slipped a little while I was gone home, but I had a progress meeting with them, made it very plain that I expected them to bring their work back on schedule, even if it took working over time, or increasing their manpower. Your Company bought into his schedule when they were awarded the contract. They said they could do the work on schedule, and that is exactly what I expect you to do. After that the work seemed to speed up, but I kept watching for any sign of a slow down. After I had been there about six months. Fluor Daniel found out that the man that was Representing the Company we were constructing the building for had not fully informed Gerald of information that he needed to do the job properly. Fluor Daniel moved Gerald to another project, and brought in Dan Lyons from Fluor Headquarters in his place.

I knew Dan from talking to him on the phone, but I had not met him. When he came aboard he did things different than Gerald. I`m not saying that he did things wrong, I `m merely saying that he did them differently. We all had to learn to do things his way, and that took a little time, but we did learn his way quickly. Things began to get back to normal, and we were soon back on, schedule. Then a 7.1 Earthquake hit the Bay area, doing damage from Santa Cruz up to Oakland where the top lanes of I -880 fell down on the lower lanes crushing cars, and trapping people in their cars, some were trapped for several says. Then it Continued across the bay bridge causing a 50 feet section to fall down on the lower level stopping traffic on both levels, and moving on into the East Bay area where several three story houses sank in the jelly like soil beneath them.

I was in my truck traveling south on Flores street near my apartment when I pulled around a double parked car, then it hit. my left front tire seemed to go flat instantly. I pulled to the left to straighten up, and my right tire went flat. Then I knew it was an Earthquake. I jammed on the brakes, and watched the electrical cables swaying dangerously back, and forth in front of my apartment. Then everything was deathly quiet. It only lasted 15 + seconds, but it seemed like an eternity. I hurried across the intersection, parked my truck, went upstairs to check on my wife, and found her to be alright, but scared. I remember that the news channel would remind us in case of an emergency, turn on your Radio, and wait for instructions, and they will tell you what to do. Guess what? The Radio was the first thing that went out. Our T. V was on cable, but there was an antenna in the attic. I unhooked the cable from the T. V. , and hooked the antenna wires to it, and it came on.

We walked around to the other apartments to check on them. No body was hurt, but our next door neighbors T.V. was laying flat on the floor. We helped her get it back on the stand, and hooked the antenna to it, she also had a picture. Then we told the other tenants that they could hook the antenna to their T.V`s and they would work. After finding that all of our neighbors were alright, we went back to our apartment and started watching T.V.to see what was going in other parts of the city. Then we saw one of the reporters on the bay bridge. She was crossing the bridge when one end of a section fell to the lower level. There were only two cars in front of her when she got stopped. She got out of her car, and started reporting what was going on around her, and it was hours before the traffic was cleared away so she could turn around, and go back to the west end of the Bridge, and find another way to go home.

When I got to the job the next morning, Dan called us all into his office, and told us we needed to walk through the building, and make a note of everything we could find that had been damaged by the Earthquake. We all went through the building together making a list of the damage that was done to the work that each superintendent was responsible for, and getting the cost from the Contractor to repair the damage, and writing a work order to cover the cost of the of the repairs, and labeled it, Earthquake damage. This put a lot of extra work on all of us, but that goes with the job. Fluor Daniel made a request for an extension on the schedule, and it was granted. It took some time, but we considered it the nature of the beast.

During the course of the job I had a problem with the transmission in my S-10 Chevrolet truck. One of the guys who worked on the job called Nona`s garage where he lived, and got a price to fix it of $600.00. which was $800.00 less than a bay area garage quoted me, so I took it to Mona`s garage, and got it fixed. We continued working on the Earthquake damage as well as doing the work that was on the schedule to begin with, and toward the end of February we were getting close to the end of the project. On march two 1990 Dan told me that my part of the job was finished, told me to go by the Redwood City office on my way home, and check out with Patty Gunderson. Dan said, he would keep checking around to see if he could find a place he could use me, and If I find anything I will get in touch with you.

I did as he said, and started getting ready to go home. The next day I rented a trailer the same size as before, and got some men from the Church to help us to load the trailer, the car, and the truck. Then we cleaned, and vacuumed the carpet, and called them to come, and inspect the apartment. When the owners arived to inspect the apartment, they were suprised to see everything so clean. They wrote us a check for the security that we put up when we rented the apartment, and, helped us load the few items in the trailer, but the vacuum cleaner would not fit into any place we tried. We gave it to them to use on the apartment complex. On this date I- 07- 0-9 we said good bye to a dear friend of ours, Doyle Wilson, just one week ago we said good bye to a dear friend Jimmy Shelnut. I wander which one of our friends will be next ?

Chapter 43

With everything loaded, I got in the truck, and Lela got in the car, and drove away, with our friends waving good bye. We got on Highway 92 that led us across the Hayward bridge, through the City of Hayward, and on out of the Bay Area. We hadn`t gone more than 80 miles when Lela called me on the walkie talkie, and said smoke is coming out from under the truck. I pulled over to the side of the road, stopped, and looked under the truck. The smoke was coming from the back of the transmission. I got back in the truck, drove on down to a small town in hopes of finding a telephone to call a wrecker service. I found a number in the phone book, dialed the number, and a man answered. I told him what my problem was, and he said I can take you anywhere you want to go. I told him where I was, and he drove up within ten minutes, with a flat bed wrecker.

He put the trailer on the flat bed, tied it down, and hoisted the front of the truck up, and said; where to ! Nona`s garage in Turlock I told him. He said you can ride with me, and motioned for Lela to follow. He knew where the place was, and drove strait to the garage, but nobody was there. He unloaded the truck near the front gate, and put the trailer in a place where it wouldn`t be in anybody`s way. He gave me the ticket, and I gladly paid the $90;00 he charged to haul us 70 miles. I left my business card on the windshield, telling them that we would be back in the morning. We drove about a mile up the street, and checked into Motel, and spent the night. We were up the next morning ate ereakfast, and drove to Nona`s garage. They were in the progress of opening up for business.

I went in, told them who I was, and what I was there for, and one of them said, we remember your truck. He went out to the truck, raised the hood. Poured some transmission fluid in it, and drove it into the garage. He hoisted it up, and looked under the transmission. Then he turned to me, and said; the back seal has failed. We can fix it, and it want cost you anything. It is still under warranty, but it may be later in the day before we get to it. I said; that's alright. We have a room in the Motel up the street, call us when it's ready. We went back to the Motel, and sat out in the lobby. We noticed that there were a lot of people milling around in the lobby. We asked one of them what was going on? He said, we are having a Square Dance convention here in the Motel. We told them that we were Square Dancers, and they asked us to join them. We said, thank you for the invitation, but we are waiting for our truck to be fixed. We may come in, and watch for a while later. The people at the garage called later in the day, and said the truck was fixed. We went down to get it, and they had already hooked the trailer to the truck. All we had to do was get in the truck, and drive away.

I drove the truck back to the motel, parked it where I could get it out of the parking lot without having to back up, and went inside the Motel, and watched the Square Dancers a while. Lela called her cousin Alene that lived in Modesto, and asked her if she, and her husband could meet us at a Restaurant nearby and have dinner, and visit with us a while. She said; we sure can! She told us the name of a restaurant nearby, and told us how to get there. We followed her directions, and found the place without any problem. They were already there, and met us at the front door. We had a good meal, and talked about what was new with each other, and who had another child, and who had died sense we had talked to them. Then we said, good bye, and went back to the Motel. We were up early the next morning ready to get on the road again. I knew we couldn't make up the time we had lost, but we might make up some of it.

We drove over to Interstate 5 which would take us through Bakersfield. Then we took a highway that would take us to Barstow where we would get on I- 40 which would take us all the way to Little Rock Arkansas. We had our little tid-bits to munch on through the lunch hour, and we didn't stop for anything except to use the bathroom or to put gas in the vehicles. When we stopped at the end of the day we had covered a lot of miles. We did the same thing three days in a row, and when we stopped the third day we were less than 100 miles from home. The next morning we had breakfast early, and got back on the road headed for Benton Arkansas. When we got within 10 miles of Little Rock we took I -430 over to I- 30 that took us to

Benton, and on to 1110 Henry st which was home. We had notified our renters that we would be home on a certain day, and we would expected them to vacate the house before we got there.

When we went into the house we expected to find it clean, but that was not the case. They had not cleaned anything. The bathtub had a dirty ring around it that had been there no telling how long, and the walls were as dirty as the bathtub. We decided to move into the little house at 1016 Banner until we could clean the floors, and paint the entire house at 1110 Henry street before we could move into it. it took us about a month to do all of that work. We moved into the big house as soon as we got that done. We were thrilled to get into the house with more room. We also had all the things that had been in storage brought down, and moved into the house. When we got everything moved in we felt like we were back home.

As soon as we got the work done, and got settled in to our home, I started running again. I would run from the house up Spangle street to Jackmon street to River street up school house hill, around the Court House, and back track down River street to my house, which was approximately two miles. That worked well for a few days, then one day when I got to school house hill my right shoulder began to hurt. I stopped for a few minutes, and the pain subsided, I started to run again, and the pain came back. I sat down on the curb a few minutes, and the pain seemed to let up a little, I decided to walk back home. After a day or two I got an appointment with Dr. Taggart for a complete checkup. When he finished he said; I didn`t find anything wrong, but I want you to come back tomorrow. I want to put you on the tread mill, and see what happens. I went back the next day, he put me on the tread mill, hooked me on to a machine, and started the tread mill. Within three minutes he stopped the treadmill, and said; you have a heart problem.

He said I don`t know how bad it is, but I want to send you St Vincents Hospital for an Arteriogram . He turned to my wife, and said; put him the car, and take him to St. Vincents Hospital. I will make the arrangements while you are on the way up there. The Ateriogram showed that I had a blockage in the left arterary to the heart. The doctor said, he had to leave for a while, but when he got back he would take me down to O.R. and take another look to see if I needed open heart surgery. Before he got back I had a heart attack while I was lying in the bed. I have seen movies where some one had an emergency, the nurse yelled [STAT]. I saw it in reality. Within seconds they were shooting morphine into me, and the attack only lasted fifteen minutes. When he got back he found that I didn`t need open heart surgery. He did angioplasty, and it lasted thirteen years. He has done three or four stints since then, and now he tells me that my heart is doing so good, that I will probably die from something else. Now I keep wondering what is [something else?]

In June of 1991 we met in Los Vegas at the home of our sister Hazel, and her husband Bill who was the host for the ninth Family Reunion since out mother passed away. We all had a wonderful week end with the family, and most of the family started back home Sunday afternoon except Lela, and I. The first year we were back home in Benton I bought a G. M. C. truck with an extended cab. I bought a plastic cover for the truck, and put an insert in the bed of the truck to sleep on, and built an extension out to the end of the tailgate, and turned it into a camper, and called it Motel 3. We had driven it out to Hazel, and Bills house, and instead of starting back home Sunday, We drove down to South San Francisco to see Ann Adams, and her husband, and visited with them a couple of days. Then we took I- 80 through northern California to Reno Nevada., and on to Winnemucca Nevada where we spent the nigh

We went to town and ate dinner in a nice restaurant When we got back, and started to get the bed fixed to go to bed I reached down behind the cushion to push it in place, and I caught my right thumb nail on a piece of metal, and turned back. Lela asked for directions to the Hospital, and took me to the emergency room. The Doctor said; the nail will have to off. It will heal better without it. He bandaged my thumb, gave me some pain medicine, and gave me a prescription for antibiotics, , and told me to get it filled when you get to the next town in the morning. when we got back to our parking space, it was about mid- night. We were up early, had breakfast, and was on I -80 headed for the first city to find a drug store where I could get my prescription filled. I got back on the freeway traveling east through the southern part of Wyoming, across into Utah where we spent the night in an R.V. Park.

We got the last space available, and it was on the back side of the camping grounds. next to a swift flowing stream We set up our table, and chairs on the bank of the stream, and ate our sandwiches as we watched the water rushing by.We really enjoyed the northern part of Utah. We took I -15 on into Colorado, and stopped at an R.V. Park in the North West corner of Colorado for the night. The next morning we were up early, and took I -70 across Kansas, and spent the night in an R-V Park in Kansas. Soon after we left the R.V. Park we got on I -35 south through Oklahoma City, and on to I -40 East, through Fort Smith, Conway, right on 430, right on I 30, on to Benton , and home. All of this time I was nursing my right thumb it was pretty sore the first two days, but after that it didn`t give me much trouble. We had a good trip, but it was good to get back home.

We did not do much of anything that first week home, but lay around, and take it easy. I had had planned to start refurbishing the house which included putting a pitched roof over the den that was the carport at one time. Adding four feet to the back of the house, and making the kitchen fourteen by twelve feet, and adding a two car carport at the back of the house. I also had new architectural grade shingles with a 40 year warranty, applied to the roof. Then I went inside, and built my wife a knew kitchen with oak cabinets through out. Then I bought a new Refrigerator, kitchen sink, a built in oven, and an under the counter dishwasher Then I had the house covered with vinyl siding. Almost everywhere we lived, while we were moving around the country, the houses had wood fences around the back yard We decided that we would like a back yard fence also. I purchased the lumber, and built the fence, and we have enjoyed the privacy we get by having a fence around our back yard.

Chapter 44

After I finished the house, and the back yard fence I began helping Ralph with his home repair business. He had contracted to refurbish a house for a lady in west Little Rock, and needed help. In addition to myself, my brother Dale, and his son Mark came to help also. We started at the ground, and worked up. It was a big house, and it took something like eight months to do the job. While we were working on the house, I read in the Benton courier that the mayor had hired an Electrical Inspector, and would probably hire a building inspecter in the near future. I called the Mayor, and told him I would like to be considered for the job of building inspecter. He said, you will be first in line when I get ready to hire. A few weeks later the Director of community Services called, and asked me to come up to City Hall for an interview. I went up to his office, and gave him my resume to look at, he looked it a minute, and looked up at me, and said, I think we need you more than you need us. We will call you to come to work soon.

We were about finished with the house when the Mayor called me, and said; can you come to work tomorrow; I said; I will be there. I started working for the City September third 1993, and after working there a year I was elevated to Building Official in charge of issuing building permits, doing all building inspections, and HVACR inspections on both residential, and commercial buildings in the city of Benton. Before I went to work for the city I advised the Mayor that I had volunteered to go to Australia with a group of people to help build a church there. He said, you go ahead, and plan to do that. We will have someone to fill in for you.

When the time came our group left Little Rock at 8;40 AM, and landed in Dallas. We changed flights there, and flew to Los Angles, where we had to carry our luggage across the Airport to board the plane that would take us to Australia. Take my advice, do not take two much carry on luggage! This plane was the biggest I have ever been in. It had three seats on each side, and seven in the middle area. We arived in Sydney about 12;00- 0 clock Australian time.The flight time was 14 hours. We had to check through customs there, and again in Brisbane which was another hours flight. Then we had to wait for the busses to get there to take us to the camp where we would be staying for the next two weeks. By that time Glenn Turner and I had become Buddies. Brother White, his Wife, and several others met us at the Brisbane Airport. It was three A. M. when We arived at Neranwood which is a youth Center run by the United Church youth Conference. We lost Thursday because of the time difference. By the time we all found a bed to sleep in, and got a bath it was four A. M. Glenn Turner, Darrell Perryman, Michael Forest, Doug Smith, and myself wound up in the same cabin. The Youth camp is set in a valley overshadowed by Eculyptus, Gum, and Bay trees. We had a huge building with a Kitchen in one corner, with tables and chairs. This is where we ate breakfast. Then We all got on three busses, and went to a bank in Mudgeeraba to get our money exchanged.After that we went to the Gold Coast where we had lunch at a huge Sizzling Steak house. We went from there to an Animal Sanctuary where we saw all kinds of Birds, Kangaroos, Kulha Bears, Ostrich`s, and others I can`t name. While we were there I bought a Camera to replace the one I lost in Dallas.

We spent part of the day at the Church attending the morning Services, and then we went to a Mall where Glenn, and I bought some gifts. I purchased some opal ear rings for Lela, an opal tie pin for myself, and an opal neckless for each of my daughters. Then we went to the Gold Coast, and had a picnic at the Beach, and it was similar to the Beaches in California, but a lot hotter. A lot of the Business places do not have air Contitioners, and the youth camp didn`t even have a fan. The heat was almost unbearable . We worked the first day at the Church on Monday and it was quiet an experience. Nobody knew where to start, but it more or less worked itself out. We all had a tendency to gravitate to the type of work that we were familiar with. Then the remainder joined different groups. I asked Brother white what Glenn, and I could do! he said; can you hang doors? I said; that`s what I do best!

He took us down to the basement, showed us where the doors were stored, and asked what tools we would need? I had brought a set of wood chisels, hammer, screw drivers, and other miscellaneous tools with me. Then I gave him a list of tools that we especially needed for hanging doors. Glenn told me that he didn't know anything about hanging doors, but if you will tell me what to do, we will get the job done. The first thing I did was to build a door jack to hold the door while I worked on it. I told Glenn to keep the tools close to where I was working, and set a door beside each door opening. After a while everything began to come together. Glenn began to put every thing where I needed it before I was ready for it, and that was good. We soon were able to speed up the process, and soon we had hung all the doors that was on the jobsite, and had to go back to building window frames until more doors were delivered to the jobsite We continued hanging doors until we had all of the doors in the building hung. Then we went back to work on the window frames. When they were all, finished, and in place, we helped anybody that needed help.

Tuesday January the eleventh. It started raining during the night, and continued raining for the better part of three days. When we went back to the jobsite the thirteenth we found 12 inches of water in the basement. We swept water all morning, and it finally quit raining about noon. The rain had caused us to loose at least two days work, and we couldn't afford to loose much more time. We are already working more hours each day mostly in the evenings, and eating at the jobsite. At this point I want to congratulate all of the Church women who worked diligently to feed us at noon, and again in the evening. I also want to give Venessa a gold star for bringing us water every thirty minutes. I don't think I would have made it without the water. The fact that we were working late each day kept us from getting to the Youth camp until 8:30 or 9:00 o-clock in the evening, but we had time for conversation in our cabin. We had a very good group in our cabin. Glenn was always razzing Darrell about what he is going to tell Angie when we get home.

We worked today until about 3 P.M. putting window frames together, and erecting trusses. Then we attended A barbeque at Allen Jones's house, and had a wonderful time. This family is Australian, and were very Hospitable. These People are very friendly People. Brother

White preached a good Sermon We ate lunch at Mc. Donolds, and two buses` full went to Timberline Mountain, and went through the rain forest. It rated right up there with everything else we had seen there. We went back down the Mountain to the church, and had a good evening Service. Then we ordered Pizza, went back to the camp, and ate it there. Monday the 17 th- 1994 We continued framing outside walls, Hanging trusses, and installing window frames. Two other guys, and myself finally got to play Golf. We played two rounds on a 9 hole coarse. The coarse wasn`t that great, but I just wanted to play a round of Golf in Australia. Tuesday Jan, 18-1994, we finished hanging doors, and started installing window frames, and other miscellaneous items.

Jan. 19. 1994. We all went to the jobsite, but we didn`t get to work because of rain. Some went shopping for last minute items. Part of us went back to the jobsite, others stayed to do more shopping. It was still raining, and the only people working were building pews down in thbasement We gathered at the, Dining hall for the evening Service that turned into a Testimonial Service. Everybody testified, and it was as a great Service. Thur. 20. 1994 it was 4. A.M, and the only ones up was Darrell, and myself. It was still raining, and had been raining all night. We all had to do some last minute Packing, and we had to clean up the cabin before we got on the Busses to go to the Airport to catch the plane to Sydney. We had delays at every Airport on the way home, but we made better time than we did going over there because we had a tail wind coming back To sum it up, the past two weeks has been a great experience. Both physically, and spiritually. We met good people from other states, and the people we met in Australia, were so warm and friendly. I will never forget it.

Chapter 45

Monday morning after I got home I went to work, and found my desk covered with telephone messages. It took me the better part of the day to answer all of my calls, but after a day or two everything got back to the same old grind. Of course at that time of the year there was not as much building going on as there is in the summer months, but I had plenty to do. I also had a few Contractors that didn`t like the idea of having to get a permit for small buildings like storage buildings, but there was no one that really knew the ordinances well enough to tell them Which ones that needed a permit, and which ones that didn`t need a permit, but It was all there, all anyone needed to do was to get the ordinance, and read it, and apply it, and enforce it. Even then some didn`t want to comply with the ordinance. I had to take a few to court to make believers of them. Was I too tough? No I don`t think so. I was doing what I was getting paid to do.

Soon after I got back from Australia, I was at a family gathering, and Linda, a sister of Lela`s made a statement, that she had recently joined the Saline County Toastmasters Club. I responded with, what is Toastmasters!? She answered, Toastmasters is a club that teaches people how to improve their Communication, and leadership skills. Where do they meet, I asked? At the saline County Hospital Cafeteria Conference room. What time do they meet? Each Wednesday at twelve 0-clock noon she answered. I couldn`t wait for the next Wednesday to come. I had heard of Toastmasters, but I had no idea what they did. I thought maybe they taught people how to give a Toast, but I found out that was far from the truth. At Wednesday noon I drove to the Hospital, parked the car, and walked inside, and Linda was there waiting for me. She said, lets go through the Cafeteria,and get our food , and go on into the meeting room. We eat while we are having the meeting. There were several people already there. She introduced me to them, when we were all seated one of the Members walked up to the Lectern, and opened the meeting. Then we stood up for Prayer, and pledge of Allegiance. Then he asked Linda if she would introduce her guest. She introduced me, and everyone acted like I was a very important person. You would have thought I was the President of the United States. I was impressed by the attention was getting .

As the meeting progressed, some of the members gave speeches, and some evaluated the speeches. Then there was one that was called the ah counter, and another that was called the Grammarian that graded everyone on their Grammar. They timed everything that anyone did. I watched the Timer as he worked, and wondered how he could keep up with the amount of time that everyone took on the things they did. Then the Toastmaster of the meeting asked him to give a report on the time that everyone took on everything that they did during the meeting. I thought, there is no way I could ever do that. After the meeting was over, they asked me if I would like to join the Club? I said, "I surely do."

They signed me up right then, and there, and gave me a starter manual which had ten speeches to choose from, and suggested that I do # one first, called the ice breaker because it is about yourself, and nobody knows you as well as you do. Then they asked me if I would like to do it next week? I said ; Why not? I gave my Ice breaker the following week and everybody said; I did great, but I was scared to death. I continued giving speeches ever two or three weeks, and within a year I had completed all ten Speeches in the Manual. Then I was awarded the C.T.M. award, Competent Toast Masters. Then I was given the A.T.M. Advanced Toast Masters Manual that had five speeches in it. Each speech was more defficult, and required more time to prepare, and took more time to complete, therefore becoming an impact on the progress.

Even though I was impacted by the slower progress, I was able to advance through the advanced Bronze, Gold, and silver, before I came to the proverbial point of no return. I had not given much thought as to how far I would pursue the art of improving my communication, and leadership skills. It seemed that I had come to the point, that I needed to make a decision to either quit where I was , or go for the gold, so to speak. I talked to Joyce Moore who had come to us from another Club, and had gone to the top, and had been given the D.T.M.

Distinguished Toast Masters award. Which is as far as you can go in Toastmasters. I asked her what I should do? She said, I think you should go for it, and I will tell you why. You have done especially well up to this point, and I think it would be a shame for you to waste the time you have put on it up to this point. I think you should go for it, and I will help you every of step of the way. I said, that`s the best offer I have ever had, then I said; I will go for it.!

With her help I continued through, one Manual after another, studying Leadership techniques, and achieved the Competent Leadership award. Served a complete term as Area Governor, Completed the High Performance Leadership program, served successfully as a club Sponsor, or Mentor, and was awarded the D.T.M. Distinguished Toastmaster, award which is the highest award given in Toastmasters. I was the first, and only member to achieve this award in our Club. I am still a member of the Saline County Toastmasters club, Even though I don`t attend the meetings as often as I should. At this point in time I have been in Toastmasters fourteen years, and I intend to stay in Toastmasters. Through speech writing I have learned the art needed to write this book, and I give toastmasters full credit for that.

In the meantime I continued working for the City of Benton until 2002, When I retired for the second time. I guess I`m a glutton for punishment. I like to keep busy. I joined the fitness Club in the early nineties, and I still try to work out three days a week. My only claim to fame is, when I did a Commercial along with several others for a Mexican restaurant in North Little rock. They had me seated at a table opposite a nice looking woman. Every now, and then a guy would walk up beside me and say in a low voice, I saw your Commercial, and then say, that wasn`t your wife setting across the table from you, was it? I would whisper, no but she knows it wasn`t her. I wasn`t my intention to be boastful about everything I have done. I have always tried to have a positive attitude about everything I had the pleasure of doing, therefore I put all of myself into any, and everything I did to accomplish whatever I was doing.

About five years ago I was appointed to a five year tenure on the Board of Trustees at the Hershfield Memorial Library. I am in the process of serving my last year as the Chairman of the Board. Lela, and I have been Married sixty two years. We have two Daughters Diane

Prokos, and husband Charles Shephard who has three sons, Chris, Paul, and Jon, and Debbie Tully, and husband, James Tully who has two daughters Jill Hawkins, and husband Chad Hawkins who has a son Tristen, and daughter Zoey, and Julie Gunter, and husband Todd Gunter who has a daughter Ashton, and a son Colton. That makes us a total of 15 Grand Children. When we all get together at one place , there is a bunch of us.

Chapter 46

Two years ago this coming February nineteenth at about seven o-clock in the morning, Lela noticed that I wasn`t up  yet, and that wasn`t normal. I was usually up at five o –clock. She came in to check on me, and found that I was not only unable to get up, I wasn`t able to tell her what was wrong with me. She dragged me out of bed, and stood me up, and some how got me into the Den, sat me in my chair, and, called 911, and asked them to come, and get me. They rushed me to the hospital, and into the emergency room. They tell me that I was talking out of my head, and was unaware of my surroundings. When the Doctors finished their examination, they found that I had 103 Degrees of fever, Type B influenza, along with ear infection, and a ruptured ear drum. After further observation the Dr. determined that I also had Bacterial Meningitis. I was immediately transferred to the I.C.U. unit. I had been in a coma since entering the emergency room.

Four days after I was admitted to the Hospital I was still in a coma. Doctor Hill made an evening visit to my room. After going through his usual procedure. Debbie asked him? Is there anything else we can do to bring my Daddy back to us? He said, there is only one thing that will bring your dad out of this now, and said; that`s why I came over this evening. He placed his hand on my head, and began to pray for my healing, and wisdom for him to know how to take care of me according to Gods will. That, and the fact that people in churches all across the county were praying for me also, and I think that was responsible for what happened next. Dr. Hill came in the next morning, walked by my bed, and said,; "good morning, Ray," and I said Good morning, Dr. Hill." I believe with all my heart that I was in god`s`shands the night before, and god decided that he needed to keep me here a while longer.

I don`t know what he kept me here for, but I am convinced that he will reveal it to me when he is ready for me to know. I have been a

Christian since I was 22 years old. I have tried to live a life that people would know that I am a Christian without having to tell them. If there are any of you out there that does not know Jesus Christ as your personal Savior, I urge you to get down on your knees, and pray for him to save your soul, and he will. Then you need to be baptized in a local church, and become a member of that church, and attend church Services as often as you can. There are some people who believe they can live a good life, and their works, will take them to Heaven, but it doesn`t work that way .Jesus died on the Cross to pay for all our sins, but you have to ask him to save you. Now that is not too hard to do, is it?

After I came out of the coma I was transferred to a regular floor where some of my family could stay with me at all times. Then I was transferred to the Rehab unit where my family could only visit from 3 P. M. TO 8 P. M. I still had some tough medical problems to deal with. I developed a very painful staff infection on my chin, sores in my mouth, making it defficult to eat or drink, herpes simplex [virus] in my left eye, and a tube was put in my left ear due to the ear infection witch ruptured my ear drum causing the Bacterial Meningitis. By the time I got to rehab I had lost 20 pounds, and could barely get out of bed without assistance. I do remember two of my Grand Sons Paul and Jon coming to see me from Kentucky, and Alabama. I was so glad to see them.

During the first few days in Rehab I was so tired, and sleepy I wasn`t sure what was going on around me. The Nurses, and Nurses aids would come by now, and then to bring me medication, or something to eat or drink. Dr. Cash would come by almost every morning to see how I was doing, and talk about golf. I really enjoyed having him come by to spend a little time with me. I could hardly believe my wife when she told me how long I had been in the Hospital, and all the ailments I had contracted since I had been there. I told her I was so sorry that I had caused her so much worry. I think I loved her right then more than I had ever loved her before.

After I caught up on my sleep I went to the gym with the help of my Therapist, Fredrick Hansen. He started me out very slowly, doing easy exercises, and gradually increasing the resistance as my body got stronger to the point that I began to look forward to going to the gym.

I have so many people to thank for helping me get well. I want to thank all the Doctors, all the Nursing staff, and all the Rehab Staff, for having patience with me when all I wanted to do was go back to sleep, all the Home Health Nurses, and Therapist who came to visit me two times a week for two weeks after I came home, and told me that I didn`t need them anymore, and recommended that I be approved to go to the Saline County Hospital out patient gym for training designed to get me in condition to play Golf.

Most of all I want to thank Debbie, and James, for being with us all the way. James was there every time we needed him, and Debbie was with her mother every day, and every night. I don`t know what we would have done without them. I also want to thank God for all the people in my church, and other churches across the country who prayed for my recovery. I only weighed 148 when I was discharged from the Saline County Hospital, worked with home health two weeks, and Larry worked with me three weeks in the out Patient gym getting me in shape to play Golf. Two years later I have gained back to 173 pounds, and try to work out three times a week. I am 83 years old, and all of my Brothers, and sisters are still living. The oldest is my Brother Ralph who was 90 in Nov. and the youngest is my Brother James who was 72 in August. I have lived a very interesting life, and I thank God for it.

The End

I want to thank my Wife for being so patient with me while I sat at my Computer two to four hours each day, for the past twelve months, composing what I consider an interesting part of my life She has read each paragraph of what I have written, and has suggested changes where ever she thought was necessary, and I have given in to most of them. She has been a wonderful, wife, a good mother to our two daughters, and has supported me in everything I attempted to do. Without her encouragement this Book might not have been written.

I want to thank Clay Ford ,who grew up in a fine family next door to us on Henry Street, in Benton Arkansas. My wife and I had just moved back to our house at 1110 Henry St from San, Mateo California. We watched Clay, and his brother Cody grow up. I got to know Cody first. He would stand in the window, and call to me, what chu doin Mister Draddy? I would answer, I`m working on the yard. We were referred to as Mister Wilson, and Dennis the Mennis. I would ask him once in a while, where is your brother Clay? And Cody would say. In there on the computer.! I am so thankful that he spent most of his time in there on the computer, otherwise this book might not have been finished and published. Thank you so much Clay, for coming over anytime, day or night, to fix my computer.